# VIENNA

Philippe Bénet
and
Renata Holzbachová

J·P·M
PUBLICATIONS

# Contents

## Light and Shadow

The Viennese pendulum swings forever back and forth between dream and reality. The name conjures up a vision of waltzes and operettas, of revolutionaries and artists imagining new worlds in cosy coffeehouses, of lovers hurrying away from a Schubert piano recital to sip new wine in a *Heuriger* wine garden.

This is all still true. But Vienna is also a town of hardheaded businessmen leading a thriving economy into the new Europe.

The bowler-hatted cabby who trots his horse-drawn *Fiaker* past the Hofburg imperial palace delights in telling endless romantic tales of the Vienna Woods, of the trysts and suicides of wayward Habsburg archdukes and their mistresses and other lovers. And the taxi-driver threading his Mercedes through the noonday traffic on the Ringstrasse takes equal pleasure in his cynical spin on the latest crisis in the neighbouring Balkans or another corruption scandal on the Vienna Stock Exchange.

The town provides the obvious setting for one of its most illustrious sons, psychoanalyst Sigmund Freud, to have dissected the dreams that reveal the sombre side of man's and woman's unconscious. Darkness and light are everywhere. Yes, the Viennese are charming. The effect is accentuated by the melodious flow of their language. But the charm may also be accompanied by an undercurrent of sometimes malicious irony, the notorious *Wiener Schmäh* (Viennese sarcasm), that can catch the visitor unawares. Just take it as the spice of life, like the *Kren* (horseradish sauce) that adds a sharp touch to the celebrated Austrian delicacy, *Tafelspitz*—boiled beef. Without this keen ironic edge, the distinctive atmosphere of *Gemütlichkeit*, the snug warmth that is the city's preferred mode of life, might be insufferably cloying.

## At the Heart of Europe

Since the collapse of the Soviet bloc and the entry of Austria into the European Union in 1995, Vienna has resumed its historic role as an important and increasingly active player in relations between eastern and western Europe and as an informed and experienced observer of the Balkans.

A glance at names in the telephone book shows, besides

the dominant community whose German language prevails, the varied origins of its citizens—Czech, Slovak, Polish, Hungarian, Italian, Turkish and representatives of all the states of former Yugoslavia. Enriched by their culture, language and cuisine, the town is full of descendants and more recent immigrants from the twelve nations whose 50 million inhabitants made up the Austro-Hungarian Empire until its break-up in 1918. Naturally enough, this has led to Austria championing the entry of its neighbours into the European Union. In classical Viennese style, the government is moved by the sentiment of historic ties, almost as much as by the notion that it is good for business.

**Cradle of Culture**
In an Austrian population of some 8 million, Vienna numbers over 1,5 million. The city is both national capital and, as the *Land Wien*, one of the nine states (*Bundesländer*) of the Federal Republic of Austria. It is divided into 23 districts (*Bezirke*) covering a total surface of 415 sq km (160 sq miles). The town is surrounded by extensive forests—the Vienna Woods of which Hugo von Hoffmannsthal told his famous Tales—and vineyards providing

the early wine for those *Heuriger* wine gardens. The Danube crosses the northeastern suburbs, but only in our imagination, thanks to the waltz of Johann Strauss, is the river ever blue.

The city prides itself on its rich creative tradition—the streets "paved with culture, as the streets of other towns are paved with asphalt," declared writer Karl Kraus at the beginning of the 20th century. Streets and monuments alike, concert halls, Opera House and Burgtheater, the imperial palaces of Hofburg, Schönbrunn and Belvedere, are laden with the greatest names of Europe's musical, literary, artistic and architectural traditions: composers Brahms, Beethoven, Mozart, Haydn, Schubert and Strauss, more recently Mahler, Schönberg and Webern; writers Schnitzler, Zweig, Musil and Thomas Bernhard; painters Klimt, Kokoschka and Schiele; architects Adolf Loos and Otto Wagner. And the city is at last paying due tribute to Freud, quite as much great writer as pioneering scientist.

**The Coffeehouse**
The second Turkish siege of Vienna in 1683 had two happy consequences. The Ottoman armies were repelled, but they left behind the noble art of

coffee making, which the Viennese turned into a whole way of life.

Business, pleasure and romance all begin or end in a Kaffeehaus. The choice for the appropriate place is endless. The bourgeoisie plumped for the delicacies of Demel, the imperial café and pastry shop, or its rival in the Sacher hotel. Painters have discussed their new works in the Hawelka. Writers made their second home in the Griensteidl, Alt-Wien, Prückel or Central.

Waiters work at a leisurely pace, so don't get impatient. Try a cake or fruit tart with whipped cream, or read one of a dozen international newspapers hung out for you on a central table. Get to know one of the many kinds of coffee: *Mélange* with milk, *kleiner Schwarzer* an espresso, *Einspanner* black coffee topped with whipped cream, and each served with a glass of cold water.

**One, Two, Three, One...**
Vienna has five seasons—after spring, summer, autumn and winter, the ball season. Grand balls are held throughout the *Fasching* (Carnival) from November 11 to Ash Wednesday. The haunting music of Johann Strauss recalls images of Emperor Franz Joseph opening the dance with his Empress Sissi. Today the Ball still has its formal place in Vienna's winter programme. Ladies put on a long dress, gentleman don white tie and tails or at least a dinner jacket. And the dance goes on till 5 a.m., when the coffeehouses provide an appropriate *Katerfrühstück* (literally "hangover breakfast"). With scarcely time to change into work clothes, people then go off to the office.

Sons and daughters of the Old Vienna aristocracy still learn their steps at the dance schools, most famous of them the Thomas Elmayer, preparing them for the waltz and foxtrot at one of the more prestigious events like the *Juristenball*, the Lawyers' Ball. Equally appreciated are those of the pastry-chefs, the hunters or the policemen. The most glorious, however, is the Opera Ball. Every year, on the Thursday before Shrove Tuesday (Mardi Gras), the *crème de la crème*, all 7,000 of them, gather to dance, to see and be seen. Young ladies all in white have practised their mazurka, polka and waltz and now venture out onto the gleaming parquet floor of the State Opera. The Master of Ceremonies formally opens the ball with the words "Alles Waltzer"— "Everybody waltz!" Join in.

# Flashback

The Vienna region has been inhabited since prehistoric times and was always coveted because of its geographical position. Celts lived here in the 4th century BC and were driven out by the Romans some 300 years later.

The outpost of Vindobona (Celtic: "White Field") which developed into Vienna took on great significance because neighbours to the north were interested in using the Danube as an important trade route. Emperor Marcus Aurelius died here in AD 180. As the power of the Roman Empire declined, Vienna was frequently invaded by barbarians and finally destroyed around 400. It was subsequently occupied by a Germanic tribe from Bavaria.

Towards the end of the 8th century, Charlemagne incorporated the Ostmark (East March) with Vienna into his European empire. Within a hundred years, the Magyars had conquered the region from Hungary.

Retrieved by the Babenberg dynasty, the lands were inherited by the newly created Holy Roman Empire in 976. The name Austria *(Ostarrichi)* first appeared in 996 in a document signed by Emperor Otto III.

## Birth of Austria

Over the next three centuries, the empire expanded under the Babenbergs. In 1156, Emperor Frederick I made the East Mark a duchy with Vienna as its capital. Henry II moved his court from the Leopoldsberg, a nearby hill overlooking the Danube, to what was to become the Hofburg palace.

The town grew in beauty. A new city wall was built with the ransom money paid for King Richard the Lionheart. The Austrians had captured him in 1192 on his way home from the Third Crusade. Vienna soon became a centre of trade and culture, with a population of over 10,000.

After a victory over the Hungarians in 1246, Emperor Frederick II fell from his horse and with him went the Babenberg dynasty. Austria passed to Bohemia, and the Holy Roman Empire stayed without an emperor from 1254 to 1273. Finally, Rudolf I von Habsburg was elected German king, and the House of Habsburg ruled Austria till the end of World War I.

## The Habsburgs

Rudolf asked Ottokar II of Bohemia to hand back Austria.

After the Bohemian king's death in battle at Marchfeld, Austria returned to the Holy Roman (German) Empire in 1278. Four years later, Rudolf I gave his sons Albrecht and Rudolf the fiefdoms of Austria and Styria (Steiermark).

The Habsburgs wanted to elevate Vienna to the ecclesiastic rank of bishopric. In the early 14th century they began to build St Stephan's cathedral in place of the Romanesque church consecrated in 1147. In 1365, Duke Rudolf IV founded the University of Vienna, second oldest university in the German-speaking world, after Prague (1348).

Duke Albrecht V von Habsburg became king of Hungary in 1437 and a year later king of Bohemia. With the name Albrecht II, he made Vienna the capital of the Holy Roman (German) Empire.

After the death of his brother Albrecht, Frederick III was the last German emperor who had himself crowned in Rome. The crown was now hereditary and Austria was elevated in 1453 to rank of archduchy. During civil insurrection in 1462, the Viennese citizenry besieged the Hofburg for two months, with the emperor and his family barricaded inside.

Inaugurating Austria's matrimonial policy, which reached its climax under Charles V, Frederick III arranged the marriage of his son Maximilian I to Mary of Burgundy, who brought as her dowry the earldom of Burgundy and the Netherlands. Matthias Corvinus, King of Hungary, coined the phrase: *"Bella gerant alii, tu felix Austria nubes"* ("Let others wage war, you, happy Austria, get married.")

Maximilian I, King of Rome and German Emperor, set about reorganizing his empire. After declaring what are now Austrian federal states to be "hereditary lands", he was obliged to make compromises with the German princes who refused centralization. Thus were created, among other things, the supreme court and the chancellory.

In 1515, Maximilian I celebrated in St Stephan's cathedral the double wedding of his grandson Ferdinand and granddaughter Mary with the children of Ladislas II, king of Hungary and Bohemia. Consequently these lands became part of the Habsburg empire.

After his death, his grandson Charles V, who already owned Castile, Aragon, the Netherlands, Naples, Sicily and Spain's overseas possessions, became German ruler. He reigned from 1519 to 1556 over an empire that embraced half of Europe.

The ideas of the Renaissance gained ground throughout the continent and the Reformation spread through Germany, much to the displeasure of the emperor.

## Turkish Sieges

Soon another danger threatened the empire. Sultan Suleiman the Magnificent occupied Hungary and laid siege to Vienna with an army of 120,000 in September 1529. Count Niklas Salm's garrison of 20,000 soldiers resisted the attacks and forced the Turks to retreat. Nonetheless, the danger of a Turkish invasion remained for another 150 years.

After the abdication of Charles V, his brother Ferdinand I, already heir to the thrones of Bohemia and Hungary, became ruler of Austria in 1556. Eight years later, he was succeeded by his son Maximilian II. Although he supported the Catholic Counter-Reformation of the Jesuits, he also called for tolerance and promoted the Reformation movement. Under his rule, some 80 per cent of the population converted to the Protestant faith. Ruling from 1576, his son Rudolf II guaranteed the Protestants freedom of worship.

At the beginning of the 17th century, however, the Counter-Reformation triumphed. In the Thirty Years' War (1618–48), the town was threatened by the Bohemian army in 1619 and the Swedish army in 1645. Three years later, the Peace of Westphalia put an end to the confusion.

Vienna had scarcely recovered from the plague of 1679 when the Turks returned to besiege the city. In 1683, Grand Vizir Kara Mustapha massed a force of 200,000 men at the city gates. The 15,000 troops of Count Rüdiger von Starhemberg were powerless to stop the destruction of the city outskirts. It was only the heroic intervention of Prince Eugène of Savoy that finally forced the Ottoman armies to withdraw. For his loyal services he was rewarded with the two Belvedere palaces and a winter residence in the Himmelpfortgasse.

With the Turkish menace out of the way, Vienna started an intensive programme of construction, which gave the town much of its baroque character. Aristocrats of the Schwarzenberg, Kinzky, Lobkowitz and Lichtenstein families built splendid mansions around the city centre. At the same time, new buildings for the Hofburg, court library, Spanish Riding School and imperial chancellory were added. The jewel of Viennese baroque was the grand Karlskirche built for Emperor Charles IV by Johann and Joseph Fischer von Erlach. Under Empress Maria Theresa (1740–80) the Habsburgs completed their summer residence, the opulent Schloss Schönbrunn.

## Maria Theresa

Karl VI, who had no son, secured his succession by what the European royal courts acknowledged as the Pragmatic Sanction. His daughter Maria Theresa took over the government in return for her husband François renouncing his duchy of Lorraine. Nonetheless, after the death of Karl VI in 1740, the empress had to defend Habsburg possessions during an Austrian war of Succession that lasted eight years. The Treaty of Aachen confirmed in 1748 the Pragmatic Sanction and Maria Theresa could at last concern herself with legislative and administrative reforms and diplomacy. She bore 16 children, among them her heir Joseph II, and Marie Antoinette who met an unhappy end in the French Revolution.

Vienna became the capital of European music; its most famous composers included Joseph Haydn and Wolfgang Amadeus Mozart.

Joseph II was crowned emperor after the death of his father in 1765, but had to share power with his mother. As an enlightened ruler he wanted to transform his empire into a modern state: he opened up to the whole population the hunting grounds of the Prater and Augarten, hitherto reserved for the aristocracy, fought privileges, introduced civil marriage and promulgated an edict of religious tolerance. At the death of Joseph II, Austria was weakened, but less because of these reforms than through the resistance they provoked.

## Napoleon in Vienna

In 1792, war broke out between Revolutionary France and Austria. Franz II was the last Holy Roman (German) Emperor (1792–1806) and at the same time the first hereditary emperor of Austria under the name Franz I (1804–35).

In 1805, Napoleon launched a new offensive on Austria and occupied Vienna. The following year, Franz I renounced his crown, and the Holy Roman Empire was dissolved. Vienna revolted in 1809, and Napoleon was defeated at Essling but was victorious two months later at Wagram. During his second occupation, the French emperor had the city shelled for 24 hours on end. Many paintings from the imperial gallery in the Belvedere were carried off to France. The composer Haydn, old and feeble, died of grief, even though Napoleon had him tended by his personal bodyguard.

Napoleon lived out at Schönbrunn and visited the town only at night, by torchlight. His marriage to Maria Luise, daughter of Franz I, took place in the Augustinerkirche in 1810. She bore him a son, the Duke of Reichstadt and King of Rome, who died of tuberculosis at 21.

After Napoleon's abdication, the Congress of Vienna assembled numerous princes and statesmen who worked out a new order for Europe under the influence of the arch-conservative Austrian chancellor, Prince Metternich—between dances at the Hofburg palace.

The subsequent quiet years of the stolid Biedermeier period proved a glorious era for music: Beethoven and Schubert created immortal works, Johann Strauss father and son conquered the world with their melodies. But political oppression and police dictatorship led to the revolution of 1848. From March to October, insurrection grew, culminating in the assassination of the war minister. Chancellor Metter-

nich fled Vienna. Ferdinand I, son of Franz I, was forced to abdicate and was succeeded by his 18-year-old nephew, Franz Joseph.

**Franz Joseph and Sissi**
While the empress felt very close to the Hungarian people, Franz Joseph was much beloved among the Viennese. Under his long reign (1848–1919), the capital took on its present-day appearance. From 1857, fortifications were removed and replaced by the broad boulevard of the Ringstrasse, with imposing buildings like the Parliament, City Hall and University. Vienna's cultural life took on a new lease of life. The Staatsoper (State Opera) opened in 1869, the Volksoper (People's Opera) in 1898; followed by the Musikverein and other concert halls. From 1891, the famous art and science museums were opened to the public. Spacious parks brought the town more greenery, and the city was modernized with a tramway, the Urania planetarium and the Prater's giant ferris wheel.

But Franz Joseph's reign was also marked by personal tragedy: his unhappy marriage to the lovely Sissi; the tragic death of his brother Maximilian, shot by revolutionaries in Mexico in 1867; the suicide of his son and heir Rudolf, with his mistress, in 1889; the murder of his wife by an Italian anarchist in 1898 in Geneva, and finally the assassination in 1914 of his nephew Archduke Franz Ferdinand in Sarajevo, which led to World War I.

At the same time, several crises beset the Austro-Hungarian Empire and hastened its dissolution. The dual monarchy guaranteed Hungary more independence in 1867; only the foreign, finance and war ministries were shared with Austria. Despite his will to hold the empire together, Franz Joseph was confronted with the demands of several national minorities. Participation in the alliance system of the German Chancellor Bismarck enabled him to continue on an international level until the end of the 19th century, but Franz Joseph's efforts to dominate the Balkans finally led to

---

### SISSI: MYTH AND REALITY

In the 1950s, the cinema drew a picture of Sissi that was kitschy and divorced from all reality. Empress Elisabeth (1837–98) was an intelligent and cultivated woman who worried little about court etiquette and much about the destiny of the Hungarian people. She spent a long time in the vicinity of Budapest. The sensitive empress was very much concerned about her physical appearance. For this she imposed iron discipline with exercise and a constant diet. From her 30th birthday, she refused to let herself be photographed.

After her marriage with her cousin Franz Joseph at the age of 16, she had to exchange a hitherto fairly free life in Bavaria for the strict supervision of her mother-in-law, Sophie, who also later took over the education of the children. The empress fell ill and took refuge in the milder climate of Madeira— the first of a long series of journeys abroad.

In June 1867, her efforts for more recognition for the Hungarian people reaped their reward. The imperial couple were crowned King and Queen of Hungary: the dual monarchy was born. Even this, however, did not keep Sissi in the palace. After she had given her husband four children, she decided at 40 to distance herself still further from court and pursue her passion for poetry and travel.

The empress suffered a terrible blow with the suicide of her son, Rudolf. In 1889, the heir to the throne took his life, along with that of his mistress, Baroness Mary Vetsera, on the royal estate of Mayerling. Nine years later, when out walking on the Quai du Mont-Blanc in Geneva, Elisabeth was stabbed to death by the Italian anarchist Luigi Lucheni.

the collapse of the Austro-Hungarian monarchy.

## End of the Empire

Vienna numbered 2 million inhabitants in 1910. After the assassination of Archduke Franz Ferdinand, Austria's policy of alliances drove the land headlong into World War I. In the capital, food was rationed because Hungary refused to support the war effort. Currency devaluation ruined the propertied classes.

Franz Joseph died in 1916, aged 86. His grandnephew Karl I succeeded him and was forced to abdicate and leave Austria in Novembe, 1918. The last emperor died four years later in exile on the island of Madeira. A republic was pro claimed. In 1919, the Saint-Germain and Trianon treaties sealed the fate of the dual monarchy and prohibited annexation *(Anschluss)* to Germany.

## Red Vienna

The disproportionately large capital of the shrunken state of Austria came under the influence of the Social Democrats, who remained in power till February 1934. The "red" government effected considerable achievements in the areas of health and social welfare. A new style of social housing created new neighbourhoods on the city outskirts. However, tensions grew between the bourgeoisie and the government. A workers' demonstration in July 1927 ended with the burning of the central courthouse and bloody street-battles.

The consequences of the worldwide economic crisis exacerbated radical tendencies and led in 1934 to civil war between democrats and fascists. Chancellor Engelbert Dollfuss enacted an authoritarian Christian constitution. During an abortive Nazi Putsch, the chancellor was assassinated in July 1934. His successor Kurt von Schuschnigg clung with difficulty to power until he was forced by Hitler to resign in March 1938.

## Anschluss (Annexation)

After the German invasion in March 1938, Austria became part of the Nazis' Third Reich, with the enthusiastic support of a large part of the Austrian population. Viennese citizens —Social Democrats, Communists and Jews—were among the first to be deported to the concentration camps of Dachau (in Bavaria) and Mauthausen (on the Danube east of Linz). Many others joined the SS and became active members of the Nazi Party. Between

1938 and 1945, some 6,000 citizens were executed in Vienna's city prison, thousands of others were persecuted for religious, political or "racial" reasons.

From 1943, Allied bombardment inflicted considerable damage. In the last six months of the war, more than 50 air raids caused 12,000 deaths and destroyed large areas of the city, leaving an estimated 270,000 homeless. All Danube bridges were blown up, with the exception of the Reichsbrücke. Almost all museums and architectural monuments were damaged, including St Stephan's Cathedral and the Opera House.

**The Second Republic**

In April 1945, the town was liberated by the Soviet Army and then divided up by the Allies into American, British, French and Soviet zones. During the 10 years of the military occupation, Vienna was a meeting place for spies and smugglers. (Carol Reed's film *The Third Man*, starring Orson Welles, evokes superbly the unique atmosphere of the city at this time.)

On May 15, 1955, the Austrian State Treaty gave the country its independence, along with an obligatory declaration of neutrality. The new status was celebrated with great festivities. The Opera House, Burgtheater and Spanish Riding School were ceremoniously reopened. In 1956, streets and bridges retrieved their old names, though the Viennese were obliged by treaty to maintain the Soviet War Monument on Schwarzenbergplatz.

Socialist chancellor Bruno Kreisky (1970–83) gave the city a new élan. Vienna became, not least because of its geographical situation and neutrality, the seat of several international organizations like OPEC (Organization of Petroleum Exporting Countries), the International Atomic Energy Agency and various organs of the United Nations.

In 1986, former United Nations Secretary General Kurt Waldheim was elected President of Austria, despite his wartime involvement with Nazi Germany. In recent years, the perennial government coalition of the socialist SPÖ and conservative ÖVP *(Volkspartei)* has been threatened by the ever-growing extreme right-wing party FPÖ *(Freiheiheitliche Partei)*.

In January 1995, Austria became a full member of the European Union, but it has held on to its special status of neutrality.

# City Centre

**V**ienna's landmark, St Stephan's Cathedral *(Stephansdom)*, rises from the heart of the historic 1st district that is encircled by the boulevard called the Ringstrasse. From the cathedral square, Stephansplatz, the most elegant shopping streets, Graben and Kohlmarkt, lead to the Hofburg, former imperial palace and veritable town within a town.

## Stephansdom

Subway U1, U3: Stephansplatz
Mass held Sundays and holidays
10.15 a.m., July and August
9.30 a.m.
Visit "Pummerin" bell April to
September 9 a.m.–6 p.m.;
October to March 8 a.m.–5 p.m.
Entrance to South Tower:
daily 9 a.m.–5.30 p.m.

To the Viennese, the Stephansdom, the city's landmark symbol, is known affectionately as "Steffl". It took over 250 years to build and combines several different styles. In their effort to elevate Vienna to a bishopric in the 14th century, the Habsburgs added a monumental Gothic choir to the late-Romanesque basilica dating from the Babenberg era. The original church was later destroyed but retained its west façade—the Heiden towers and Riesentor (Giants' Door)—which Rudolf IV completed with two Gothic chapels. The steeple and central nave were added in the 15th century.

At the beginning of the 16th century, a second tower had been planned for the north side, but the threat of Turkish attack diverted the money to the expansion of the city's fortifications. The Adlerturm (Eagle Tower) remained unfinished and was given a Renaissance roof in 1578. Here hangs the 20-ton "Pummerin" bell, cast from the brass of 100 captured Turkish cannons. It is only rung on special occasions, such as New Year's Day. The Stephansdom is Austria's largest Gothic edifice. The south tower, 137 m (463 ft) high, and the roof covered with 230,000 coloured tiles are visible from afar. Damage from bombs in World War II was repaired with contributions from the provincial governments. The roof is adorned with the two-headed eagle and imperial crown, and the Order of the Golden Fleece, emblem of the Habsburgs.

Accessible through the Riesentor in the west façade, the main entrance is flanked inside by two Gothic chapels. In the Tirna Chapel (left) is the tomb of Prince Eugène. The right chapel is dedicated to St Alois. The powerful nave is about 170 m (560 ft) long and 39 m (128 ft) wide. Notice the superb rib vaulting born aloft on mighty pillars.

A masterpiece of Gothic sculpture dominates the nave: the pulpit carved in 1500 by Anton Pilgram of Brno. It is decorated with rosettes, stalactites and finely sculpted leaves. Salamanders and toads symbolize good and evil. Statues of the four church fathers incarnate the four tempers—sanguine, choleric, phlegmatic and melancholy. The artist has immortalized himself peeping through a window.

Another self-portrait of Pilgram (with square and compass) decorates the foot of the organ. The exquisite "Servants' Madonna" (Dienstbotenmadonna) leaning on a pillar in front of the main altar dates from the year 1340.

On the south side of the choir, the sarcophagus of Friedrich III is a shining example of Netherlandish art. The splendid "Wiener Neustadter Altar" in the left transept was executed in 1447. Gloomy but interesting are the catacombs (entrance in the north tower), particularly the dukes' tombs of the Habsburgs.

Outside in the pavement on the south side of Stephansplatz, a geometric pattern in red tiles traces the floorplan of the Magdalene Chapel burned down in 1781.

The square directly at the corner of Graben and Kärntner Strasse is known as "Stock im Eisen" (Stump in Iron). The name refers to a tree-stump into which journeymen locksmiths drove in a nail at the beginning of their apprenticeship when they left Vienna.

## Haas-Haus

The venerable "Steffl" is reflected in the glass façade of the Haas-Haus (1985–90), first severely criticized by the conservative Viennese but now an integral part of the city-centre scene. Besides its fashionable and expensive boutiques, a first-class restaurant here offers a magnificent view.

## Around the Graben

The fortification moat from the Roman era was filled in during the 13th century, served as a vegetable market in the Middle Ages and became famous in the 18th century for the favours of its "Graben Nymphs". Today the elongated esplanade is one of the most elegant squares in Vienna, with expensive shops and open-air café terraces. In the middle stands the baroque Pestsäule (Plague Pillar) erected by Leopold I in memory of the 1679 epidemic which cost some 100,000 lives.

Even public toilets can be of artistic value, as is demonstrated by Adolf Loos's Jugendstil (Art nouveau) facilities in the middle of the Graben. Other noteworthy monuments are the baroque Palais Bartolotti-Partenfeld (No. 11), the neoclassical Spar-Casse (savings bank) building (21) and the Haus zur grünen Wiese (Green Meadows, 8) with its décor of old-fashioned cake tins, built for the pastry chefs' guild in 1705. The Anker House (10) is a work of Jugendstil architect Otto Wagner. The Café de l'Europe (31) is a legendary Coffeehouse where writers Bertolt Brecht and Franz Mehring met in the 1930s. There are many more to be explored in the side streets off the Graben.

## Peterskirche

⋮ Petersplatz

Turning right off the Graben, Jungferngasse leads over to the slender Peterskirche, whose dome was inspired by that of St Peter's in Rome. The church begun by Italian architect Gabriele Montani in 1702 was completed by baroque master Johann Lukas von Hildebrandt with two towers rising at an angle to the main structure. The interior is opulently decorated. The ceiling painting in the dome depicts the Assumption. On the left, notice the baroque pulpit of Matthias Steinl and Lorenzo Mattielli's altar dedicated to St John of Nepomuk. A loggia bears the Habsburg two-headed eagle. Ornate bejewelled shrines at altars on either side of the choir contain remains of Roman martyrs, including St Benedict.

## Kohlmarkt

This street, one of the most distinguished in Vienna, leads from the Graben to the emperor's winter residence. Charcoal fuel was sold here until the construction of the Hofburg in the 14th century. This immediately improved the neighbourhood.

It still boasts two major "monuments" of Viennese social life: the showrooms of the great Thonet furniture manufacturer, famous for its bentwood creations, especially the rocking chair; and the beautifully decorated windows of the equally celebrated pastry shop of Demel, supplier of delicacies to the imperial family since 1789 and to the rest of the sweet-toothed world ever since.

### BREEDING GROUND FOR THE ARTS

Art, architecture, literature, philosophy, psychoanalysis, cinema—there's scarcely any field in which Vienna's artists and intellectuals were not leaders in the 20th century. Nobody can speak today of the mind without quoting Sigmund Freud. Similarly, modern philosophy is inseparable from the names of Ludwig Wittgenstein and Karl Popper, and economics from that of Carl Menger. Social Democrats cite the Austrian Marxist leader Otto Bauer, the Zionists Theodor Herzl. Vienna's school of 12-tone music revolutionized modern composition, led by Arnold Schönberg, Alban Berg and Anton Webern. In architecture, Otto Wagner was an innovative force, followed by Adolf Loos and Josef Hoffmann in functionalism. The decorative painting of Gustav Klimt opened the way to the Expressionism of Egon Schiele.

The Viennese Secessionist movement grew out of a decidedly conservative atmosphere. Otto Wagner's geometric constructions were a direct reaction to the pompous monumental edifices of the Ringstrasse. Gustav Klimt attracted the support of 178 fellow painters. Artists cultivated psychological self-analysis and the quest for pure form. In 1899, *Jugendstil* (Art nouveau, but literally "style of youth") found its architectural temple, the domed Secession building, decorated with Klimt's 26-m (85-ft) long Beethoven Frieze.

## Jüdisches Museum

Dorotheergasse 11
Tel. 5350 4310
Open Sunday to Friday
10 a.m.–6 p.m. (Thursday till
8 p.m.) Closed Jewish New Year
and Day of Atonement;
open Austrian public holidays

Housed since 1993 in the
18th-century baroque Palais
Eskeles, former home of a Jewish
banking family, the museum tells
the glorious and horrific story of
Jewish life in Vienna, with a
permanent collection and
temporary exhibitions. A café and
bookshop are attached to the
museum.

## Michaelerkirche

Michaelerplatz

Across the square at the
intersection of Kohlmarkt and
Herrengasse is the entrance to the
Hofburg. Archaeological discoveries
show that this was already an
important crossroads in antiquity.
Over the centuries, the area
underwent several changes. The
Michaelerkirche now has a
neoclassical façade, but was
originally Romanesque; choir and
belfry are both Gothic. The finely
wrought entrance, 18th-century,
depicts the *Fall of the Angels*.
Besides the Romanesque nave and
side-aisles, the former imperial

parish church also has a crypt with
remains of Habsburg ancestors.
Funeral mass for Wolfgang
Amadeus Mozart was said here in
1791.

## Loos-Haus

Michaelerplatz 3

This masterpiece of sober
functional architecture by Adolf
Loos (1870–1933) caused great
controversy when it was built in
1911. The unadorned dark green
façade disappointed Viennese more
accustomed to elaborate ornament.
In protest, Emperor Franz Joseph
preferred to keep his curtains
drawn for weeks on end rather
than have to look at it.

## Bundeskanzleramt

Ballhausplatz 2

The west wing of the Hofburg
houses the Federal Chancellor's
office and the Foreign Ministry.
The Congress of Vienna held its
conferences here from September
1814 to June 1815, and it was here
that the Nazis assassinated
Chancellor Dollfuss in 1934.

## Herrengasse

This has long been a favoured
residential street for the Viennese
aristocracy. Among the palatial
mansions, look for Palais Wilczek
(No. 5), early 18th-century; Palais

*Inspect the intricacies of the Plague Pillar then take a leisurely coffee-break on the Graben.*

Modena (7), now the Ministry of the Interior; Palais Mollard-Clary (9), housing a distinguished art gallery; Palais Lichtenstein (13), erected in the 16th century and renovated in the 19th. Admire, too, the elegant entrance to Palais Ferstel, earlier home of the stock exchange. It is a maze of arcades, inner courtyards and stairways. Immediately adjacent is the elaborately renovated new home of the famous Café Central.

## Freyung

This elongated square was once a gathering place for foreigners and thieves seeking refuge in the Benedictine Schottenstift mission. It has two imposing mansions— Hildebrandt's Palais Daun-Kinsky (1716) and the 17th-century Palais Harrach on the corner of Herrengasse.

The allegorical figures of the Austria Fountain in the middle of the Freyung represent the four most important rivers of the old Habsburg Empire: the Danube, Elbe, Weichsel and Po.

## Schottenstift

The Schottenstift and Schotten-kirche were a mission and church founded in the 12th century, in fact by Irish Benedictine monks (who hailed from the Scottish island of Iona). The church is known for two 17th-century altars and a monumental tomb by Fischer von Erlach. Miraculous powers are ascribed to the 13th-century Madonna statue. The foundation also includes a renowned high school, Schottengymnasium, and a museum with painting from the 15th to 19th centuries, a highlight being a 15th-century altar painting.

## Am Hof

The inner city's largest square was the site of the Babenberg dynasty's great castle, of which all trace has now disappeared. During reconstruction of the town after World War II, Roman remains were uncovered, today exhibited in a museum (Am Hof 9). On Friday and Saturday, an antique and art fair is held here.

## Mariensäule
⋮ Am Hof

The angels on the Madonna monument that dominates the broad square represent the struggle against the four scourges of humanity: famine (the dragon); war (the lion); plague (mythological basilisk with its lethal stare) and heresy (the serpent).

## Zu den neun Choren der Engel
⋮ Am Hof

It was from the balcony of the Nine Choirs of Angels church that Franz II proclaimed the end of the Holy Roman Empire in 1806, thereby becoming the first Emperor of Austria. Among treasures in the interior: the organ, the main altar and the vault of the St Ignatius Chapel.

## Palais Collalto
⋮ Am Hof 13

Next to the Nine Choirs church, this baroque mansion is one of the city's many "Mozart addresses". It was here that the child prodigy gave his first public concert, at the age of 6.
The building at No. 10 is the old arsenal and now the palatial home of the fire brigade, topped by sculptures by Lorenzo Mattielli to the glory of the firemen. Nearby is the fire brigade museum.

## Palais Obizzi
⋮ Schulhof 2
⋮ Subway U1, U3: Stephansplatz
⋮ Tel. 533 2265
⋮ Tuesday to Sunday
⋮ 9 a.m.–4.30 p.m.

On a quiet square not far from the Nine Choirs church, this elegant mansion houses Vienna's delightful

Clock Museum. The collection boasts 12,000 items tracing the technical and aesthetic development of the clock.
Next door (No. 4) is the Doll and Toy Museum.

## Judenplatz

In the Middle Ages, this square was the centre of the Jewish quarter. Apart from a few remains of an important synagogue and talmudic school, little has survived. At the 15th-century "Haus zum Grossen Jordan", a Gothic relief depicts the baptism of Jesus. A Latin inscription recalls the destruction of the Jewish quarter in 1421, when 200 Jews were burned to death—"atoning for the terrible crimes of the Hebrew dogs". This is now countered by a statue of the great German humanist Gottfried Lessing as a lesson in tolerance, along with a new Holocaust monument currently being completed.

## Wipplingerstrasse

This long thoroughfare is graced by several baroque buildings: the Bohemia High Chancellory, a work by Fischer von Erlach; opposite, the Altes Rathaus (old city hall), which now houses archives of the Austrian anti-Nazi resistance movement. Also try to take a peek in the inner courtyard at the ornate 18th-century Andromeda Fountain, by Georg Raphael Donner, showing Perseus saving the lovely Andromeda from a sea-monster.

## Maria am Gestade

As its name suggests (Gestade: riverbank), this slender church with its open-work tower once stood beside the Danube before the river's course was diverted. It was roughly contemporary with the Stephansdom and is a major achievement of Gothic architecture. Decorating the porch are sculpted reliefs of John the Baptist and the Apostle John.
Notice inside the 14th-century stained-glass windows and the fine Gothic-era paintings portraying the Annunciation and Coronation of Mary.

## Ruprechtskirche

⋮ Seitenstettengasse
Standing on a height, the little Ruprechtskirche is the oldest church in Vienna. It is dedicated to St Rupert, the patron saint of Bavaria (650–718), whose statue stands near the entrance.
A previous building stood here in the early 8th century. Some 400 years later, a Romanesque church was built on the foundations of the first chapel. After reconstruction in the 13th

and 15th centuries, only the nave and part of the tower remain from the Romanesque era.

## Hoher Markt

This square, the city's oldest, constitutes the historic core of Vienna. Inside the house at No. 3, remains of the Roman Forum are visible. In the Middle Ages, the city market was held here—and public executions, too. In more soft-hearted times, the gallows were replaced in 1729 by the marble and bronze fountain of the Wedding of the Virgin *(Vermählungsbrunnen)*. Take a look, too, at the Jugendstil Anker Clock (set up by the Anker Insurance Co.), going through its mechanical paces since 1914. Each hour, silhouettes of Marcus Aurelius, Maria Theresa, minstrel singer Walter von der Vogelweide, composer Joseph Haydn and various other historical figures make fleeting appearances. At noon, all 12 characters sally forth, with musical accompaniment.

## Bäckerstrasse

Here the Schwanfeld House at No. 7 is worth a look for its splendid Renaissance courtyard and charming arcades. It was the home of 19th-century Biedermeier painter Friedrich Amerling. Directly opposite, Palais Seilern (8) was the Vienna home of French writer Madame de Staël. Notice on the façade of No. 12 (on the corner of Essiggasse) a charming little painting of a bespectacled cow and a wolf playing backgammon. Bars and cafés on this street are favourite night-time haunts for Vienna's artists.

## Fleischmarkt

The Schönlaterngasse, which owes its name to the beautiful lantern at No. 6, leads to the old meat market. The butchers were subsequently replaced by the Greek community. Apart from the Greek Orthodox church, the neighbourhood has long been famous for the restaurant known simply as the Griechenbeisl, which numbered among its guests Mozart, Strauss and Schubert, as well as writers Grillparzer and Nestroy. Further up the Fleischmarkt is the "Bermuda Triangle" of restaurants and bars in which Vienna's young crowd likes to get lost.

## Franziskanerplatz

This picturesque square is graced by the recently restored Franziskanerkirche and, besides the fountain, one of the town's most charming coffeehouses, a tiny place aptly named Kleines Café, famous for fried eggs.

## Winterpalais des Prinzen Eugen

Himmelpfortgasse 4

Leopold I was not lacking in gratitude. To thank Prince Eugène of Savoy (1663–1736) for his victory over the Turks, he let him draw on the services of Austria's greatest architects to build a summer residence—the two Belvedere palaces—and this winter palace in town. Begun in 1697 by Fischer von Erlach, the baroque edifice was completed in 1724 by Hildebrandt. Its ceremonial staircase is magnificent. Today the palace, in which the great soldier died, is the seat of the Finance Ministry.

## Figarohaus

Domgasse 5

Subway U1, U3: Stephansplatz

Tel. 513 6294

Tuesday to Sunday 9 a.m.–12.15 p.m. and 1 p.m.–4.30 p.m.

Wolfgang Amadeus Mozart (1756–91) and his wife Constanze lived in this pretty house from 1784 to 1787. It was here that Mozart composed *The Marriage of Figaro* in 1785. The composer's only Vienna home still in existence—where his guests included Haydn and Beethoven—has been turned into a small museum with a few of his personal belongings.

## Singerstrasse

The doorway of No. 16 is flanked by two powerful Titans who appear to be supporting the 18th-century Palais Neupauer-Breuner. The seat of the German Knights' Order, next to the Gothic Elisabethenkirche, recalls the time of the Crusades. The treasury includes relics of the Order, which is today a charitable organization.

## Rauhensteingasse

At No. 8 was the house in which Mozart died, torn down in 1847 and now replaced by the Steffl department store. When Mozart moved in here with his wife Constanze in 1787, *The Marriage of Figaro* had just scored a great triumph in Prague. But the death of his father, long journeys, debts, intrigues and the Viennese public's bad reception for *Don Giovanni* and *Così fan tutte* left the composer completely exhausted. Sick and lonely, he died of a fever in the night from December 4 to 5, 1791. His body was buried in a mass paupers' grave in the St Marx cemetery.

## Kärntner Strasse

Named after one of the nine federal states, this bustling pedestrian-zoned shopping street links Stephansplatz to the Opera House.

It is lined with open-air cafés, fountains and lime trees. Many of the houses were built after World War II.

At No. 37, the Gothic Malteserkirche was founded by the Order of Maltese Knights at the time of the Crusades and their wars against Arabs and Turks.

The venerable glassware shop at no. 26, J. & L. Lobmeyr, was built here in 1823 to serve the imperial court and now houses a glassware museum.

Further on in the direction of the Opera House is the monumental 19th-century Hotel Sacher, whose pastry shop produces the original chocolate Sacher-Torte.

## Annagasse

The Annakirche dates back to the 15th century and was subsequently modified. A sculpture in the interior portrays St Ann with Mary and Jesus. A fine ceiling painting of the 18th century is the work of Daniel Gran.

Annagasse has several important mansions—at the corner of Kärtnerstrasse, the 17th-century Palais Esterházy, now housing a casino; Hildebrandt's 18th-century Palais Deybelhof (8); and various imposing monastic "hostels": the 17th-century Kremsmünsterhof (4), Mariazell (5), and the baroque

Herzogenburgerhof (6). Notice, too, the grand façade of the early-19th-century Haus Zum blauen Karpfen (House of the Blue Carp).

## Neuer Markt

Heading down Kärntner Strasse towards the Opera, turn right on Donnergasse to Neuer Markt, where the grain-merchants did their trading. At the centre of the square is the baroque Donnerbrunnen, also known as Providentia Fountain (1739), by Georg Raphael Donner. Four statues symbolize the Danube's tributaries, the Enns, Traun, Ybbs and March. In 1873, bronze copies replaced the originals, fashioned in lead and now exhibited in the Belvedere's Baroque Museum. Among the square's handsome façades are Palais Rauchmiller (No. 14) and a 19th-century merchant's house with fine three-storied gable (10–11).

## Kapuzinerkirche and Kapuzinergruft

⁞ Neuer Markt
⁞ Crypt, daily 9.30 a.m.–4 p.m.
The extremely simple Capuchin Church was chosen by Emperor Matthias and wife Anna to serve from 1633 on as the mausoleum for Habsburgs. In 1989, almost all of Europe's royalty and, of course,

faithful Viennese monarchists took part in the funeral of the last Austrian empress, Zita, who was laid to rest 67 years after the death of her husband Karl I.

In nine crypts, the 138 coffins of the imperial mausoleum contain the remains of 12 emperors, 16 empresses and more than 100 archdukes and their wives. Particularly opulent is the rococo sarcophagus of Maria Theresa and her husband François. Countess Fuchs-Mollardt, the family tutor and personal friend of Maria Theresa is the only "outsider" buried here. Among the great absentees: Karl V, buried in Spain; Marie-Antoinette, guillotined in Paris in 1793; her son Louis, who died in France in 1795; the Duke of Reichstadt, Napoleon's son who died in Schönbrunn but whose ashes are in Paris; Archduke Franz Ferdinand and his wife; and the last emperor, Karl I, buried on Madeira.

## Palais Lobkowitz

Lobkowitzplatz 2
Subway U1, U3: Stephansplatz
Tel. 5128 8000
Tuesday to Sunday 10 a.m.–5 p.m.

This splendid late-17th-century baroque palace has a fine porch added by Fischer von Erlach in 1710. In the mid-18th century, the Lobkowitz family, patrons of Beethoven, purchased the palace. It was here that his Third "Eroica" Symphony was performed for the first time, in 1803, and his Fourth Symphony in 1807. Today, the palace houses the collections of the Austrian Theatre Museum.

---

### VANITY, ALL IS VANITY

The Habsburgs performed a strange burial ceremony. Before the funeral, the heart of the deceased was brought to the crypt of the Augustinerkirche, the entrails to the crypt of the Stephansdom. After mass in the cathedral, the coffin was transferred to the Kapuzinergruft. The Imperial Marshal, speaking in the name of the deceased, had to knock at the door of the Kapuzinerkirche, whereupon the priest asked him: "Who are you?". The court official might then answer: "I am Your Majesty, the Emperor of Austria and King of Hungary."

"I know him not," replied the priest. "Who is demanding entry?" "I, Emperor Franz Joseph, Apostolic King of Hungary, King of Bohemia, King of Jerusalem," the Imperial Marshal responded. After entry was again refused, the Imperial Marshal knelt down and replied: "I am Franz Joseph, a poor sinner and beg the grace of God." Only then was the coffin allowed in.

# The Hofburg

The strategic heart of the empire expanded in proportion to the growth of the Habsburgs' power. The ten buildings of the Hofburg express the most varying architectural styles: Gothic, Renaissance, baroque, rococo and neoclassical.

## Kaiserappartements

- Michaelerplatz 1
- Tram 1, 2 D or J: Burgring
- Subway U2: Babenbergerstrasse or Herrengasse
- Tel. 5217 7404
- Daily except Tuesday 10 a.m.– 6 p.m., museums till 4 p.m.

From Michaelerplatz, you enter the Hofburg through the splendid wrought-iron archway of the Michaelertor (St Michael's Gate). Its sculptures symbolize the mottoes of the Empire: Franz Joseph's Union of Powers; Maria Theresa's Justice and Pardon; Joseph II's Courage and Example.

To reach the state rooms and the imperial silver and tableware collection (Hofsilber- und Tafelkammer) you pass under the vaulted gate of the Imperial Chancellory (Reichkanzlei).

The Leopold Wing is the seat of the President of Austria and not open to the public.

The tour begins with the private apartments of Franz Joseph, a series of spacious chambers with Bohemian crystal chandeliers and gilded stucco, the walls hung with tapestries. In the long dining room decorated with Flemish tapestries, the table is set for a family dinner. After the meal, the emperor would accompany his guests to the Cercle reception room or the smoking parlour with its tapestries from Brussels. Official audiences took place twice weekly. Franz Joseph would stand behind his desk to hear his petitioners. The conference room reserved for his ministers, in Napoleonic Empire style, is next to his dressing room. In comparison to the other rooms, the emperor's sleeping quarters are modest: over a simple iron bed hang portraits of his wife Elisabeth and his mother Sophie.

In the adjoining Amalienburg, a Renaissance building of the 16th century, are the apartments of Elisabeth. Here you can see, beside her bedroom and living room, the gymnasium which she had made out of a dressing room, complete with wooden exercise apparatus fixed to the ceiling. When Sissi was in the palace, the royal couple dined in the splendid Grand Salon. A few of her personal effects have been kept in the small salon nearby. In the rooms which Tsar Alexander I occupied during the Congress of Vienna are memorabilia of the last imperial couple, Karl I and Zita.

## Schatzkammer

A superb Renaissance gateway, the Schweizertor (1552), opens onto the Schweizerhof courtyard.

The imperial jewels are displayed here in the Treasury: the crown of the Holy Roman Empire created in the 10th century, the Austrian imperial crown of the 17th century and the treasure of the Burgundians (15th century). Among the numerous other precious jewels, reliquaries and works of art is the magnificent necklace of the Order of the Golden Fleece founded in 1429.

## Neue Burg

In the central colonnade of the newest section of the Hofburg are three museums. The Ephesus Museum, exhibiting the Austrian excavations in Anatolia at the beginning of the 20th century, is a must for archaeology buffs. There's also an exhibition of armour and weapons, and a collection of historic musical instruments.

In the Ringstrasse wing of the Neue Burg, the Ethnology Museum has assembled over 150,000 objects from all over the world, among them the collection of Captain Cook which Emperor Franz I bought in London in 1806. Noteworthy is the elaborate feather head-dress and costume of Aztec emperor Montezuma, killed by soldiers of conquistador Hernán Cortes in 1520.

It was from the balcony of the Neue Burg, before thousands of rapturous spectators, that Adolf Hitler proclaimed the Anschluss on March 14, 1938.

## Winterreitschule

Performances of the Spanish Riding School: April to June, then September and October 10.45 a.m.–7 p.m., lasting roughly 90 minutes. Information on public shows: tel. 533 9032. Across Josefsplatz, the Winterreitschule is the section of the imperial stables reserved for the Spanish Riding School. The famous performances of the Lippizaner horses take place in a splendid dazzling white hall with a colonnade designed by Fischer von Erlach in 1735. The hall also served as a setting for many ceremonial occasions, notably in the Congress of Vienna. In 1814, Beethoven conducted a concert here with more than 1,000 musicians.

## Redoutensaal

The grand ballroom built in 1760 forms the right wing of the school's ceremonial hall. It was here that

---

### HIGH SCHOOL

Early in the morning, the white Lippizaner horses emerge from their stables for rehearsals across the street from the palace. The Viennese are very proud of their Spanish Riding School, which dates back to the 16th century. Archduke Karl, brother of Maximilian II, owned lands in northern Slovenia. In the town of Lipizza, near Trieste, he set up a stud to cross-breed Berber and Arabian horses brought from Spain. In 1920, after the dissolution of the Empire, the Lippizaner stud was moved to Piber, near Graz, in Styria. The training of the horses begins at the age of 4, when the coat is slowly turning white. The actual schooling begins at 7.

The Lipizzaner Museum in the Stallburg, open daily 9 a.m.–5 p.m., relates the history of the famous horses through paintings, photographs and films, from their introduction to Vienna to the present. You can also look around the stables.

the emperor held his most illustrious galas and where aristocratic delegates to the Congress of Vienna danced for weeks on end to celebrate victory over Napoleon. After a devastating fire in 1992, which practically destroyed the stables of the Riding School, too, it has been restored to its former grandeur.

## Österreichische Nationalbibliothek

The precious collections of the imperial library include books and manuscripts dating back to 14th century. The national library is one the most important in the world. The main entrance offers a splendid view over the surrounding monuments (museums, parliament, city hall). Used today for exhibitions and concerts, the great hall on the first floor (Prunksaal) is a masterly baroque design (1726) by Fischer von Erlach. The ceiling painting in the dome depicts the apotheosis of Karl VI.

## Augustinerkirche

⋮ Augustinerstrasse 3
⋮ Daily 10 a.m.–6 p.m.,
⋮ Sunday 1–6 p.m.
The former imperial parish church, built in the 14th century, was used for weddings. A painting in the left aisle, *Virgin of the Snows*, patron

saint of the House of Habsburg, was said by popular superstition to grow darker when the dynasty was threatened by misfortune. There is a fine marble monumental tomb (1805) designed by Antonio Canova for Archduchess Marie Christine, a daughter of Maria Theresa. In a crypt near the Loretta Chapel—known with characteristic sentimentality as the Herzgrüftl (little heart crypt)—54 silver urns are kept for the hearts of the Habsburgs. The urn of the Duke of Reichstadt (Napoleon's son) is decorated by a ribbon of the French tricolor.

## Albertina

⋮ Augustinerstrasse 1
⋮ (Undergoing restoration)
Historically, the home of the world's greatest graphic art collection includes literally hundreds of thousands of drawings, water colours and prints by Leonardo da Vinci, Dürer, Rubens, Raphael, Michelangelo and Rembrandt, but also 20th-century artists such as Klimt, Schiele and Rauschenberg. The Austrian Cinémathèque *(Filmmuseum)* continues to show art films here, and temporary Albertina exhibitions are held at the Akademiehof, Makartgasse 3 pending re-opening of the museum, planned for 2002.

# The Ring

Our description of monuments along the broad semi-circular boulevard called Ringstrasse goes anti-clockwise, from the University to the Danube Canal. The street is 4 km (2.5 miles) long and 56 m (184 ft) wide.

## Universität

⁝ Dr Karl-Lueger-Ring 1

The University of Vienna was founded in 1365. You can still visit the original Science Academy (Akademie der Wissenschaften, Dr-Ignaz-Seipel-Platz 2).

In 1883, architect Heinrich Ferstel was commissioned to build the new University in neo-Renaissance style. More than 50,000 students work here today.

## Votivkirche

⁝ Rooseveltplatz 8

Another major work of Heinrich Ferstel, the neo-Gothic church right behind his University, was commissioned by Archduke Maximilian, future Emperor of Mexico, as an act of thanks for his brother's escape from an assassination attempt in 1853. Maximilian was himself killed by Mexican revolutionaries in 1867,

12 years before the church was completed. Inside is the tomb of Count Niklas Salm, commander in chief at the first Turkish siege of 1529.

## Beethovenhaus-Pasqualatihaus

Mölkerbastei 8
Subway U2: Schottentor
Tel. 535 8905
Tuesday to Sunday
9 a.m.–12.15 p.m. and
1 p.m.–4.30 p.m.

Born in Bonn, Ludwig van Beethoven (1770–1827) came to Vienna in 1792, was a student of Haydn and soon found recognition among his fellow musicians and the Vienna public. This house, now a museum, frequently served as Beethoven's home between 1804 and 1815. He composed here the opera *Fidelio* and his 4th and 5th Symphonies.

## Neues Rathaus

Rathausplatz 1
Guided tours Monday, Wednesday, Friday (except during council meetings and public holidays) at 1 p.m.

The New City Hall is the seat of regional and city government. It was built in 1883 in neo-Gothic style by Swabian architect Friedrich von Schmidt. The spire, nearly 100 m (328 ft) high, is topped by the statue of a knight, familiarly known as the "Rathausmann". A popular restaurant, the Wiener Rathauskeller, occupies the basement.

The square in front of the Rathaus is always lively, in winter with an enchanting Christmas market or on the skating rink, in summer with the festival of opera films.

### IMPERIAL GRANDEUR

The Ringstrasse is an achievement of Emperor Franz Joseph. Impressed on his visit to London by Britain's Great Exhibition of 1851, he wanted to give his own capital a whole new look. From Christmas 1857, he had the city walls razed to make way for a broad boulevard. The Ring was bordered by numerous public buildings in different styles. The architecture was to correspond to the function. This "historicism" gave Vienna a distinctly bourgeois appearance: the Opera House, the Art and Natural History Museums and the Burgtheater recall Renaissance Italy, the homeland of art and science. Parliament resembled a Greek temple. The neo-Gothic City Hall had an English look to it. To pay for the public works, remaining prime building sites on the Ring were sold to aristocrats for their town mansions.

Refreshments are constantly available at open-air booths—hot grog *(Glühwein)* and pancakes *(Palatschinken)* in winter, beer and sausages in summer.

## Burgtheater

- Dr-Karl-Lueger-Ring 2
- Tel. 514 440
- Guided tours July and August Monday, Wednesday and Friday at 1, 3 and 5 p.m.
- From September to June by advance reservation.

Empress Maria Theresa founded the first Burgtheater in one of the Hofburg's ballrooms. In 1874, construction began on a new Burgtheater, opposite the Neues Rathaus. It opened in 1888. The building designed by Carl Hasenauer and Gottfried Semper in Italian Renaissance style was destroyed in 1945 but fully restored after the war. The Viennese claim it is in the Burgtheater that the German language is spoken at its best.

## Parlament

- Dr-Karl-Renner-Ring 3
- Tel. 401 100
- Guided tours Monday to Friday (except debate days) 11 a.m. and 3 p.m.

The Danish architect Theophil Hansen completed the edifice in 1884. A student in Athens, he designed the parliament building in neoclassical style in honour of the cradle of democracy. It was here that the dual monarchy was dissolved and the founding of the republic proclaimed. The bicameral parliamentary system has a national council *(Nationalrat)* elected for four years and the federal council *(Bundesrat)* comprising representatives of the nine federal states.

## Naturhistorisches Museum

- Maria-Theresien-Platz
- Subway U2: Volkstheater
- Tram 1, 2 D or J: Dr-Karl-Renner-Ring
- Tel. 521 770
- Daily except Tuesday 9 a.m.–6 p.m.

Across from the Hofburg are twin buildings housing two museums, one devoted to Natural History, the other to the History of Art (Kunsthistorisches Museum, see below). Dominating the square between the two is the imposing monument to Maria Theresa. After the Burgtheater, architects Hasenauer and Semper tackled both these buildings in Italian Renaissance style.

Departments of the Natural History Museum are devoted to prehistory, anthropology, mineralogy, zoology and palaeontology. The particularly fine collection of precious stones includes a topaz weighing 117 kg (257 pounds). Also famous is the 25,000-year-old limestone statuette known as the *Venus of Willendorf*, a fertility symbol unearthed at the beginning of the 20th century in Lower Austria.

## Kunsthistorisches Museum

- Maria-Theresien-Platz
- Subway U2: Babenbergerstrasse
- Tram 1,2 D or J: Burgring
- Tel. 525 240
- Paintings: daily except Monday 10 a.m.–6 p.m.; Thursday till 9 p.m.
- Egypt, Orient, Antiquity, Sculptures and Coins: daily except Monday 10 a.m.–6 p.m.

One of the greatest in the world, the History of Art Museum displays the Habsburgs' collections assembled over the ages and finally opened to the public by Franz Joseph at the end of the 19th century. The rich collection of paintings is up on the first floor. It exhibits Flemish, Dutch, Italian, French, Spanish, English and German masters, including Arcimboldo, Brueghel, Dürer, Poussin, Rembrandt, Rubens, Raphael, Titian, Tintoretto, Velazquez (portraits of the Spanish royal family) and Vermeer, whose *Allegory of Painting* is one of the museums most prized possessions.

On the ground floor are the Egyptian, Oriental, Greek and Roman art treasures and sculptures. The coin collection is on the second floor.

## Staatsoper

- Opernring 2
- Subway U4: Karlsplatz
- Tram 1, 2 D or J: Oper

Franz Joseph commissioned August Sicard von Sicardsburg and Eduard van der Müll to build the Opera House, a neo-Renaissance temple of lyrical art. At its opening in 1869, it came under violent attack from the Viennese who found it ugly and unworthy of the city's musical heritage. In 1945, it was badly damaged, but restored to its former appearance—without too much criticism—and reopened in 1955 with Beethoven's *Fidelio*. On the Thursday before Mardi Gras, the opera house is transformed into a giant ballroom for the traditional annual Opera Ball.

## Stadtpark

- Parkring
- Subway U4: Stadtpark
- Tram 1, 2: Weihburggasse

The city park, which stretches across both banks of the Wien Fluss canal, was the first public park to be opened by the municipality, in 1862. Statues of Viennese musical celebrities include Schubert, Bruckner and Lehar. The gilded monument of Strauss, the violin-playing Waltz King, is a favourite photo subject for tourists. Concerts are held from Easter to October at the Kursalon bandstand near the park entrance.

## Museum für angewandte Kunst (MAK)

- Stubenring 5
- Subway U3: Stubentor
- Tram 1 or 2: Dr-Karl-Lueger-Platz
- Tel. 711 360
- Daily except Monday 10 a.m.–6 p.m. Thursday till 9 p.m.

The Museum of Applied Arts was built from 1867 to 1871, originally as the museum of art and industry. It was followed a few years later by the School for Applied Arts next door, with its brightly coloured façade.

The museum, reopened after extensive renovation in 1993, is above all a show-place for the celebrated Wiener Werkstätte (Vienna Workshops), but also for collections of 800 years of handicraft, design, utensils and other practical objects from all over the world.

The exhibition rooms organized chronologically were designed by well known contemporary artists such as Jenny Holzer, Franz Graf or Donald Judd. Make sure you see the Jugendstil collection, comprising chairs and other furniture, coffee sets, and so on. Don't forget to call in at the museum's trendy MAK-Café.

## Postsparkasse

- Georg-Coch-Platz 2
- Tram 1,2 or N: Julius-Raab-Platz
- Monday to Friday 8 a.m.–3 p.m., Thursday till 5.30 p.m.

The building of the Postal Savings Bank, the first modern edifice on the Ringstrasse, is a fine example of the architecture of the Vienna Secession movement. It was built in 1906 by Otto Wagner, pioneer of functional aesthetics, and to this day it has lost none of its avant-gardism. Otto Wagner also designed part of the building's interior furnishings which are still in use.

## Urania

- Uraniastrasse 1
- Tram 1, 2 or N: Julius-Raab-Platz

On the Danube Canal, with two façades looking onto the water, this Jugendstil building designed by Max Fabiani, a disciple of Otto Wagner, was erected in 1910. It houses an observatory, a cinema and several lecture rooms. In the observatory is a telescope for amateur astronomers.

DER·ZEIT·IHRE·KVNST·
DER·KVNST·IHRE·FREIHEIT·

# Karlsplatz and Belvedere

A walk from the Opera over the Ring shows a good cross-section of Vienna architecture: the 19th-century Hotel Imperial, the characteristic Jugendstil Karlsplatz subway station, and the baroque Karlskirche. Further south is the Belvedere and its splendid gardens and museums.

## Karlskirche

- Karlsplatz
- Subway U4: Karlsplatz
- Daily 8 a.m.–7 p.m.,
- Sunday 9 a.m.–7 p.m.

Vienna's finest baroque church is dedicated to St Charles Borromeo, Bishop of Milan (1538–84). His statue crowning the pediment was sculpted by Lorenzo Mattielli. St Charles had showed great courage when Milan was struck by the plague, and after Vienna was hit by the same disaster, in 1713, his example prompted Emperor Karl VI to have this monument built by Johann and son Joseph Fischer von Erlach. The grandiose edifice epitomized the power of the Catholic Church and of the Habsburgs. With a formidable copper dome flanked by two triumphal pillars covered in spiral bas-reliefs, it is one of the city's great landmarks. When the U4 subway line was dug, the whole square in front of the church was transformed. Henry Moore donated one of his sculptures to the city and it now graces a monumental pond in the square.

## Historisches Museum der Stadt Wien

- Karlsplatz
- Subway U1, U2, U4: Karlsplatz
- Tel. 505 8747
- Daily except Monday
- 9 a.m.–4.30 p.m.

Opened in 1959, the City of Vienna History Museum traces the development of Vienna from prehistoric times to the 20th century.

## Hotel Imperial

- Kärntner Ring 16
- Subway U4: Karlsplatz
- Tram 1, 2: Schwarzenbergplatz
- Tel. 5011 0333

Vienna's most distinguished hotel lives up to its name—guests are treated like emperors. Drink a coffee in the lounge to get a feeling for the refined atmosphere. Built as a palace for the Duke of Württemberg in 1865, it was transformed to a grand hotel for the World Exhibition of 1873.

## Musikvereinsgebäude

- Bösendorferstrasse 12
- Subway U4: Karlsplatz
- Tram 1, 2: Schwarzenbergplatz
- Tel, 505 8190
- Open September 1 to June 30

Venerable home of the Vienna Philharmonic, the building was commissioned by the Gesellschaft der Musikfreunde (Society of Music Lovers) from Theophil Hansen, Danish designer of the Austrian Parliament.

Behind its distinctive ochre façade, completed in 1869, are two concert halls: the Brahmssaal for chamber music and the famous Goldener Saal, known throughout the world for its New Year's Day concert by the Vienna Philharmonic. All the concerts are sold out well in advance.

The gilded caryatids and other sumptuous décor are repainted each summer.

## Karlsplatz-Pavillons

- Karlsplatz
- Subway U1, U2, U4: Karlsplatz
- Daily except Monday from April to October 9 a.m.–12.15 p.m.
- and 1 p.m.–4.30 p.m.

At the beginning of the 20th century, Otto Wagner was commissioned to build bridges and stations for the new municipal railway, part underground, part ground-level. He tackled the job with great enthusiasm, putting his personal stamp on the city. The success of his enterprise is admired to this day. One of the "pavilions", superbly decorated in marble and gilt, leads to the Karlsplatz subway. Another has now been converted into a coffeehouse. Other surviving stations and bridges can be seen on line U3 (Schönbrunn station) and along the Gürtel ("beltway", line U6).

## Akademie der bildenden Künste

- Schillerplatz 3
- Subway U4: Karlsplatz
- Tel. 588 160
- Tuesday, Thursday, Friday 10 a.m.–2 p.m.;
- Wednesday 10 a.m.–1 p.m. and 3–6 p.m.; Saturday, Sunday, public holidays 9 a.m.–1 p.m.

Contemporary artists develop their talents in the Academy of Fine Arts, designed in 1876 by Theophil Hansen, architect of the parliament and Musikverein. The art gallery, exhibiting works of Flemish and Dutch masters of the 17th century, is well worth a visit. You will see Rembrandt, Rubens, Van Meytens and Vermeyen, but also the literally fantastic *Day of Judgment* by Hieronymus Bosch. Painted in oils on wood panels, the great triptych

(1504–8) depicts the fallen angels, the creation of Eve, and the momentous events of the Garden of Eden.

## Secession

- Friedrichstrasse 12
- Subway U4: Karlsplatz
- Tuesday to Friday 10 a.m.–6 p.m.
- Saturday, Sunday and public holidays 10 a.m.–4 p.m.

Designed in 1898 by Joseph Maria Olbrich, a major disciple of Otto Wagner, this landmark building broke with Vienna's academic artistic traditions. The exhibiting artists were rebels against the ponderous, pompous official style of their times.

The open-work dome consists of 3,000 gilded laurel leaves. An inscription in gold over the entrance sums up the philosophy of the Secession movement: "To each age, its art, to art its freedom".

In the basement is the *Beethoven Frieze* (1902) by Gustav Klimt. It is 26 m (85 ft) long and honours the composer and his 9th Symphony. Today the Secession is devoted to exhibitions of contemporary art.

## Belvedere

- Prinz-Eugen-Strasse 27
- Tram O, 71: Rennweg;
- Tram D: Gusshausstrasse
- Tel. 7984 1580

*The Belvedere: a study in perfect symmetry.*

Museums: daily except Monday 10 a.m.–5 p.m.
Gardens: daily sunrise to sunset.

After France's Louis XIV had refused him command of a regiment, Prince Eugène of Savoy entered the service of Emperor Leopold I and soon distinguished himself as a successful field commander. Thanks to his victory over the Turks in the Balkans, Austria was able to recapture Hungary. Leopold rewarded the prince generously with lands just outside Vienna city centre. Eugène's festivities found an appropriately opulent setting in the Upper Belvedere completed in 1721 by Lukas von Hildebrandt in French baroque style. After his death in 1736, his niece sold the two Belvedere palaces to the emperor. Sixty years later, the daughter of Louis XVI and Marie-Antoinette spent three years here when released from prison in Paris. At the end of the 18th century, the art gallery was installed in the Belvedere. During the French occupation of 1809, it served as an army hospital and the director of the Louvre had 401 paintings transferred to Paris. Most were returned to Austria in 1815, after the Congress of Vienna.

From 1894, the palace was the residence of the ill-fated Archduke Franz Ferdinand.

The Austrian State Treaty was signed in the Marble Hall on May 15, 1955, re-establishing Austria's independence and its neutrality. Between the Upper and Lower Belvederes are the elegant gardens laid out with statues, fountains and water basins by Paris landscape architect Dominique Girard.

## Unteres Belvedere

The Lower Belvedere served as Prince Eugène's summer residence; he settled there after the capture of Belgrade in 1716. The courtyard is reached through a handsome triumphal gateway. The palace now houses the Baroque Museum, exhibiting major Austrian painters and sculptors of the 17th to 19th centuries. Its many ceremonial halls include the Marble Gallery (Marmorgalerie), the Gold Cabinet (Goldkabinett), where a statue of Prince Eugène is reflected countless times in huge gold-framed mirrors, and the Hall of Grotesques (Groteskensaal), with a picturesque collection of grimacing heads by Franz Xaver Messerschmidt (1736–83). The walls are painted with frescoes by Jonas Drentwett depicting mythical beasts inspired by murals of ancient Rome.

In the adjoining Orangerie, the Museum of Medieval Austrian Art includes some fine altar-paintings of the 15th century.

## Oberes Belvedere

Entrance to the Upper Belvedere is through an elegant wrought-iron gateway flanked by two lions. The rococo décor reflected in the ornamental pond recalls the grand masked balls and fireworks displays which Prince Eugène loved to stage for his guests. Memories of his victories over the Turks are evoked by the elongated roofs resembling tented military camps and the domes on either side of the building, similar to the mosques of the vanquished foe.

Since 1953, the Upper Belvedere has housed the Austrian Gallery of the 19th and 20th Centuries. You'll find 20th-century works on the ground floor, the Secession on the first floor and the 19th century and Biedermeier period on the second floor. In the central Sala Terrena, four great white Atlantes by Lorenzo Matielli hold up the vaulted ceiling. Among the gallery's treasures is the Gustav Klimt collection, including his famous *Kiss*; works by Egon Schiele, with his harsher treatment of similar themes of love and death; Oskar Kokoschka and Hans Makart.

## Outer Districts

Vienna has countless museums and galleries holding temporary exhibitions (the tourist office provides comprehensive up-to-date listings). Here we offer a selection of unusual places for lovers of music, architecture—or even psychoanalysis.

### Kriminalmuseum

Grosse Sperlgasse 24
2nd district
Subway U1: Nestroyplatz
Tram N, 21: Taborstrasse
Bus 5A: Grosse Sperlgasse
Tel. 214 4678
Daily except Monday
10 a.m.–5 p.m.
The Museum of Crime is enlivened with original photos and grisly pieces of evidence.

### KunsthausWien

Untere Weissgerberstrasse 13
3rd district
Tram N: Kegelgasse
Tel. 712 0491
Daily 10 a.m.–7 p.m.
The painter Friedensreich Hundertwasser created the bizarre design for this museum with recycled material and pieces of ceramics. There are no straight lines, and everything seems slightly

skewed. Despite its confusing style—or because of it—this small, private gallery is worth a visit.

## Wiener Strassenbahnmuseum

:: Erdbergstrasse 109
:: 3rd district
:: Subway U3: Schlachthausgasse
:: Tram 18, 72: Schlachthausgasse
:: Tel. 7909 44900
:: Early May to early October
:: Saturday, Sunday and public
:: holidays 11.30 a.m.–1.30 p.m.

The Vienna Tram Museum, located in the Erdberg District station, displays 42 trams tracing the history of this ever-popular mode of transport.

## Tabakmuseum

:: Mariahilferstrasse 2
:: 7th district
:: Subway U2: Babenbergerstrasse
:: Tel. 526 1716
:: Tuesday to Friday 10 a.m.–5 p.m.
:: Saturday, Sunday and public
:: holidays 10 a.m.–2 p.m.

The tobacco manufacturer Austria-Tabakwerke displays a collection of old pipes and smoking paraphernalia.

## Freud-Haus

:: Berggasse 19
:: 9th district
:: Subway U2: Schottentor
:: Tram D: Schlickgasse
:: Tram 37, 38, 40, 41, 42: Schwarzspanienstrasse
:: Tel. 319 1596
:: Daily 9 a.m.–4 p.m.

Sigmund Freud, the father of psychoanalysis, lived in this house for 47 years, and it was here that he treated his patients. The rooms are full of memorabilia of his life and work, including a complete reference library, his walking stick and hat. But the original couch has remained in the Hampstead home of his London exile.

When his father came to Vienna in 1860, Sigmund was just four years old. He stayed until a year after the

---

### CREATIVE RUBBISH

Painter and master of self-promotion, Fritz Stowasser literally made a name for himself as Friedensreich Hundertwasser. The Hundertwasser-Haus on Löwengasse in the 3rd district is a shining example of non-conformism and environmental awareness. For the façade, recycled bricks and other materials were used. No two windows are alike. A 5-km (3-mile) ceramic strip circles the façade and two onion shaped cupolas adorn the roof. Hundertwasser also designed a church, a spa, a motorway restaurant and a municipal rubbish-dump incinerator, in a similar style.

Nazi Anschluss of Austria, and died of cancer in London in September 1939.

## Museum Moderner Kunst

- Fürstengasse 1
- 9th district
- Subway U4: Friedensbrücke
- Tram D: Fürstengasse
- Tel. 317 6900
- Daily except Monday
- 10 a.m.–6 p.m.

The Museum of Modern Art is housed in the former summer residence of the Liechtenstein family, in the middle of a large park. This baroque palace was built by the architect who also designed their winter residence in Bankgasse, Domenico Martinelli, between 1691 and 1704.
The modern art collections take up the second floor—paintings by Klee, Léger, Kandinsky, Magritte and Kokoschka, and a small collection of sculptures by Brancusi, Giacometti and Max Ernst. The first floor is devoted to temporary exhibitions. (Please note that part of the museum is to be transferred to the new Museum Quarter being built on the Ring.)

## Schuberts Geburtshaus

- Nussdorferstrasse 54
- 9th district
- Tram 37, 38: Canisiusgasse
- Tuesday to Sunday 9 a.m.– 12.15 p.m. and 1 p.m.–4.30 p.m.

Franz Schubert was born in this house in 1797 and spent his childhood here. The house has been converted into a museum devoted to this extraordinary composer, remembered for his string quartets and *Lieder* (songs) such as *Die schöne Müllerin* or *Die Winterreise*. He died in 1828 at 31 and was buried, at his own request, near Ludwig van Beethoven.

## Zentralfriedhof

- Simmeringer Hauptstrasse 234
- 11th district
- Tram 71, 72: Haupttor
- Tel. 71901
- November to February daily 8 a.m.–5 p.m.;
- March, April, September and October 7 a.m.–6 p.m.;
- May to August 7 a.m.–7 p.m.

Nearly 3,000,000 people, more than the city's living population, have been buried in this huge cemetery. Among its many "celebrities", musicians have pride of place: Beethoven, Brahms, Schubert, Strauss, alongside countless writers, architects and artists. The majestic Dr-Karl-Lueger Church (1910) was designed by Max Hegele, a student of Otto Wagner, and dedicated to a former mayor of Vienna.

# Schönbrunn

In 1559, Emperor Maximilian acquired the land on which he built a hunting lodge. This was destroyed by the Hungarians and rebuilt by Emperor Matthias II. During a hunt, he discovered a spring that gave the present palace its name: Schönbrunn (Beautiful Spring).

## The Palace

Schönbrunner Schloßstrasse 47
13th district
Subway U4: Schönbrunn
Tram 10, 58: Schönbrunn
Tel. 811 130
April to October daily
8.30 a.m.–5 p.m.;
November to March daily
8.30 a.m.–4.30 p.m.
Guided tours (Grand Tour only) or individual tours with recorded commentary. Small Tour: apartments of Franz Joseph and Elizabeth (22 rooms); Grand Tour: includes apartments of Maria Theresa (40 rooms in all). Architecturally, Schönbrunn bridges the gap between the apparent rigour of the baroque style and the exuberance of rococo. The grand entrance gate, Meidlinger Tor,

which Napoleon flanked with his two imperial eagle-crowned obelisks, leads to a vast court of honour, Ehrenhof. Napoleon held his great military parades here. On the right is a small rococo theatre where concerts are held in summer. Marie-Antoinette danced in this theatre when she was a child and Napoleon attended performances here.

The apartments of Franz Joseph and Elisabeth and the 15 reception halls are in the palace's right wing.

The rooms are richly furnished, draped with brocade, the walls decorated with baroque panelling in beige and gold and hung with gleaming lacquerware and mirrors. Audience rooms have wood panelling from the 18th century. Franz Joseph's study has been maintained in its original condition, with its richly upholstered furniture. The emperor worked here till the day he died. The Breakfast Room is adorned with 26 flower medallions embroidered by Maria Theresa and

## HISTORY OF SCHÖNBRUNN

Like many monarchs of his time, Leopold I wanted his new palace to surpass the magnificence and grandeur of Louis XIV's Versailles. In 1683, the Turkish siege had left Schloss Schönbrunn in ruins and Johann Bernhard Fischer von Erlach was commissioned to build the new summer residence. Nonetheless, a first project was rejected as too ambitious and too costly. A "more modest" choice was made with only 1,441 rooms. Construction continued till 1730.

In order to give her court more sumptuous surroundings, Maria Theresa had the palace expanded in 1750 according to the plan of Nicolaus Pacassi. Thus the interior rooms received a new décor, new gardens were landscaped and the Empress opened in 1752 Europe's first zoological garden. On the hill overlooking the palace the Gloriette pavilion was built as a triumphal arch to commemorate the Austrian victory over the Prussians in 1757.

Schönbrunn's architecture marks the ascendancy of the more playfully ornate rococo over baroque. The glowing "Schönbrunn Yellow" of the buildings was copied throughout the empire on villas and palaces. Marie-Antoinette spent her youth here. Napoleon made it his headquarters in 1805 and again in 1809. His son, the Duke of Reichstadt, died here in 1832. Franz Joseph was born in Schönbrunn in 1830 and it was here that he died in 1916. In the palace's Blue Chinese Room, the last Habsburg emperor, Karl I, signed his abidcation decree on November 11, 1918.

her daughters. You will also see Empress Elisabeth's two dressing rooms, her bedroom and drawing rooms. The Yellow Drawing-Room is next to the little Hall of Mirrors (Spiegelsaal) in which Mozart gave one of his first recitals at the age of 6, in 1762. Maria Theresa held secret meetings in the Chinese Round Room (Chinesisches Rund-kabinett): a table rose up from the floor with a completely prepared dinner so no servants could eavesdrop on the conversations. The Halls of the Carousel and Horses lead to the grand Hall of Ceremonies in the palace's left wing. Notice the splendid rococo décor in the Vieux-Laque Room. The wood panelling of the Million Room is inlaid with 260 Indian and Persian miniatures, which cost 1 million florins. Beyond the bedroom of Franz Joseph's mother Sophie of Bavaria are a study and drawing-room hung with portraits of Maria Theresa, her husband François of Lorraine and their 16 children.

## Wagenburg

Daily 9 a.m.–6 p.m.

What was once the Spanish Riding School now houses the impressive collection of the Kutschenmuseum (coach museum). The rococo imperial coach of 1700 was drawn by eight white horses and used for weddings and coronations, the last occasion being for the young Emperor Karl I in December 1916.

## Schlosspark

Daily from 6 a.m. to sunset
Zoo: daily 9 a.m.–7 p.m.
Swimming pool: May to mid-September, daily 9 a.m.–7 p.m.

The great park covering 160 ha (65 acres) was open to all Viennese citizens, even when the emperor was in residence. Only the small gardens to the left and right of the palace were reserved for the imperial family. The park was laid out in French style in the 17th century and re-landscaped from 1750 to 1780. Ferdinand von Hohenberg designed the grand neoclassical Gloriette portico in 1775. Recently a coffeehouse was installed under the arcade. The view looking over Schloss Schönbrunn with Vienna in the background makes the climb well worthwhile. The Neptune Fountain at the foot of the Gloriette hill recalls the spring after which the palace is named. Hohenberg also placed an obelisk near the swimming pool and built the artificial Roman ruins in the park grounds. Visit the zoo, which has kept some of its baroque-style enclosures, then the Palm House with its tropical plants.

# Shopping

Popular gifts from Vienna range from craftware, embroidery and porcelain to confectionery such as the famous Sachertorte chocolate cake, *Mozartkugel* chocolate balls, and wines. There are also typical traditional waistcoats or embroidered Dirndl peasant-skirts, and all kinds of kitsch. The best—but also the most expensive—shops are on and around the Graben, Kohlmarkt and Kärntner Strasse.

## Mariahilfer Strasse
⋮ Subway U3: Neubaugasse
This bustling shopping thoroughfare in the 7th district is the home of department stores—Gerngross and Peek & Cloppenburg, a Virgin Megastore and many other international trend-setting boutiques.

## Tiroler Werkkunst
⋮ Mariahilfer Strasse 89
Traditional costumes (*Trachten*) and craftware.

## Meinl am Graben
⋮ Graben 19
Main branch of a top-class delicatessen and wine chain store

## ANTIQUES

In the numerous antique shops in and around the Dorotheergasse you will find paintings, rococo and Biedermeier (19th-century) grandfather clocks and furniture, memorabilia of the Habsburgs and countless portraits of Franz Joseph and Sissi.

that started out just as a coffee merchant.

### Zum Schwarzen Kameel
⋮ Bognergasse 5
One of Vienna's oldest shops, not far from the Graben, which counted Beethoven among its customers. Gourmet delicacies and select wines.

### Mohilla
⋮ Kohlmarkt 6
Best bet for tobacco smokers.

### Thonet
⋮ Kohlmarkt 6
This legendary furniture shop still sells its classic bentwood chairs.

### Demel
⋮ Kohlmarkt 14
In Vienna coffee has a distinctive flavour, and the blend sold in Demel's black-and-gold packets is renowned for its fragrance. You might also try the jams, with the

imperial seal still embossed on its jars, the violet-flavoured sweets, or the Sachertorte good enough to rival Sacher's.

### Loden-Plankl
⋮ Michaelerplatz 6
Home of the warm woollen felt loden coats and traditional Dirndl skirts, in the familiar olive green but also made in brown, grey and bright red.

### Musikhaus Doblinger
⋮ Dorotheergasse 10
Musical scores, books and periodicals.

### Dorotheum
⋮ Dorotheergasse 17
⋮ Tel. 515 600
Internationally renowned auction house. On the groundfloor, for people not in the mood to bid, are items sold at set prices.

### Wiener Porzellan-manufaktur Augarten
⋮ Stock-im-Eisen-Platz 3–4
Enchanting displays of delicate porcelain.

### Kunstverlag Wolfrum
⋮ Augustinerstrasse 10
Large selection of old art books, reproductions, lithos, prints, posters and postcards.

## Kaufhaus Steffl
Kärntner Strasse 19
One of the few department stores in the city centre. Recently renovated, bar and smart restaurant with fine view.

## J. & L. Lobmeyr
Kärntner Strasse 26
Charming old porcelain and glassware shop.

## EMI Austria
Kärntner Strasse 30
Large selection of CDs for lovers of classical and jazz music.

## Arcadia Opera Shop
Kärntner Strasse 40
Classical music lovers get first-class advice here for their purchases of CDs, scores and books from experienced sales staff.

## Köchert
Neuer Markt 15
Renowned jewellery shop off the Kärntner Strasse.

## Schönbichler
Wollzeile 4
Incredible assortment of the world's best teas.

## Ringstrassen-Galerien
Kärntner Ring 5-7
Elegant, luxury shopping mall.

## Naschmarkt
Wienzeile
Subway U4: Kettenbrückengasse
Monday to Friday
6 a.m.–6.30 p.m.;
Saturday 6 a.m.–5 p.m.
The oldest and biggest open-air market in Vienna. Look out for the Jugendstil buildings of Otto Wagner in the background, on the Linke Wienzeile. On Saturdays the Naschmarkt expands to include a flea market. Stalls spill over the pavements with their bric-à-brac, china, old clothes and curios.

---

### SACHERTORTE
Franz Sacher created this rich chocolate cake for a gala dinner in honour of Chancellor Metternich in 1832. Traditionally it has a filling of a thin layer of apricot jam and is often served with whipped cream. It can be ordered from Hotel Sacher, Philharmonikerstrasse 4, or by telephone, 514 560; they send it all over the world securely packed in wooden boxes. Other cafés—for example, at the Hotel Imperial and Demel—make their own claims to superiority. A story is told of an absent-minded American who left his papers in the famous hotel, forgetting both its name and its address. He sent a telegram to "Hotel Chocolate Cake, Vienna". It was duly delivered to Sacher.

# Dining Out

Viennese cuisine is a unique combination of influences from all over the old Austrian empire: Hungarian, Bohemian, Italian, Balkan and the Alps region. The result is tasty and nourishing.

## "BEISLN"

The city's equivalent of the French bistro, the *Beisl* is a cosy and relatively inexpensive meeting place to sample unpretentious Viennese specialities, wine and beer.

### Brezelg'wölb
* Ledererhof 9
* Tel. 533 8811
* Daily 11 a.m.–1 a.m.
* Reservation recommended

Charming restaurant; try to get a table in the basement. Good Viennese cuisine at affordable prices. The freshly baked pretzels are a must.

### Figlmüller
* Wollzeile 5
* Tel. 512 6177
* Daily 11 a.m.–10.30 p.m.
* Closed in August
* Terrace

Connoisseurs recommend the Wiener Schnitzel.

## Griechenbeisl

- Fleischmarkt 11
- Tel. 533 1941
- Daily 11 a.m.–midnight

This historic restaurant (founded around 1490) is admittedly very touristic, but the décor and typical Viennese cuisine make a visit worthwhile.

## Ofenloch

- Kurrentgasse 8
- Tel. 533 8844
- Daily 10 a.m.–midnight
- Terrace

One of the oldest *Beisln* in town. Clientèle not too young either.

## Oswald & Kalb

- Bäckerstrasse 14
- Tel. 512 1371
- Daily 6 p.m.–midnight

Good cuisine; one of the best frequented *Beisln* in the city.

## Plachutta

- Wollzeile 38
- Tel. 512 1577
- Daily 11.30 a.m.–midnight
- Reservation recommended
- Terrace

Regulars claim this has the best *Tafelspitz* (boiled beef) in Vienna. Elegant ambience, pleasant service.

---

**VIENNESE SPECIALITIES**

There's no escaping the *Wiener Schnitzel*: a thin slice of veal (also pork or turkey), lightly floured, dipped in egg and breadcrumbs and quickly sautéed. *Tafelspitz* consists of lean boiled beef, vegetables and sautéed potatoes, served with apple and horseradish sauce. For a change, how about a hearty goulash with dumplings *(Knödeln)*? Desserts also deserve a mention: a slice of delectable cake served with a generous helping of whipped cream *(Schlagobers)*, pancakes filled with cream or jam *(Palatschinken)* or *Apfelstrudel* (flaky pastry with apple filling).

---

## Stadtbeisl

- Naglergasse 21
- Tel. 533 3507
- Daily 10 a.m.–midnight
- Terrace

For a great meal, choose between the rustic main dining-room or the cosy basement.

## Wiener Rathauskeller

- Rathausplatz 1
- Tel. 405 1210
- Monday to Saturday
- 11.30 a.m.–3 p.m. and
- 6–11.30 p.m.

In the basement of the City Hall. The large, handsomely vaulted dining-room has a pleasant atmosphere.

## FINE RESTAURANTS

### Academie
- Untere Viaduktgasse 45
- Tel. 713 8256
- Weekdays noon–2.30 p.m. and 7–10.30 p.m.
- Closed Saturday, Sunday
- Reservation recommended

Top-class international cuisine, extensive wine-list.

### Das Triest
- Wiedner Hauptstrasse 12
- Tel. 589 1882
- Monday to Friday noon–2.30 p.m. and 6.30 p.m.–10 p.m., Saturday 6.30 p.m.–10 p.m.

Excellent Italian cuisine in a décor signed by Britain's Terence Conran.

### Do & Co
- Stephansplatz 12
- Haas-Haus, 7th floor
- Tel. 535 3969
- Daily noon–3 p.m. and 6 p.m.–midnight

International and Viennese cuisine. Elegant restaurant with unique view of Stephansdom.

### MAK
- Stubenring 3-5
- Tel. 714 0121
- Tuesday to Sunday 10 a.m.–2 a.m.

Café-restaurant of the Museum für angewandte Kunst (Applied Arts).

Handsomely painted ceiling. International and Viennese cuisine, served in summer on a pleasant terrace in the inner courtyard.

### Neu Wien
- Bäckerstrasse 5
- Tel. 513 0666
- Daily 6 p.m.–2 a.m.

Menu changes daily. Fashionable restaurant with paintings by popular Vienna artist Christian Ludwig Attersee.

### Niky's Kuchlmasterei
- Obere Weissgerberstrasse 6
- Tel. 712 9000
- Monday to Saturday 11 a.m.–midnight

Good cuisine, fine wine cellar (open to the public), original décor. Ask for *Degustationsmenü* to sample house specialities.

### Palais Schwarzenberg
- Schwarzenbergplatz 9
- Tel. 798 4515
- Daily noon–3 p.m. and 6 p.m.–11 p.m.

One of the finest hotels and best restaurants in Vienna, with a view of the palace's park. Very chic setting.

### Steirereck
- Rasumofskygasse 2
- Tel. 713 3168

- Weekdays noon–3 p.m.
- and 7 p.m.–midnight
- Closed Saturday, Sunday
- Reservation recommended

Surprisingly good value for money. Delicious food, friendly service, fine wine cellar.

## Tempel

- Praterstrasse 56 (inner courtyard)
- Tel. 214 0179
- Tuesday to Saturday
- 6 p.m.–midnight

Simple, pleasant setting for outstanding cuisine, good wine list.

## Vincent

- Grosse Pfarrgasse 7
- Tel. 214 1516
- Monday to Saturday
- 6 p.m.–midnight

Intriguing menus and good wine list. Vegetarian meals can be ordered in advance.

## COFFEEHOUSES

The Kaffeehaus has a special atmosphere that's unique to Vienna. It's a cross between a café and a restaurant, a place where you can while away a whole day reading newspapers, observing other people, playing chess, discussing—or eating cake.

## Alt-Wien

- Bäckerstrasse 9
- Daily 10 a.m.–2 a.m.

Rendezvous for night owls. The chocolate cake here is much appreciated.

## Bräunerhof

- Stallburggasse 2
- Monday to Friday
- 7.30 a.m.–7.30 p.m.
- Saturday, Sunday to 6 p.m.

Popular with writers, formerly the favourite haunt of Thomas Bernhard. Concerts Sunday afternoon.

---

### A QUICK COFFEE?

Not likely. In Vienna a coffee is to be savoured slowly, not swallowed down in one gulp. The choice is confusingly large. Here are a few explanations:

*Brauner*: black with a dash of milk.
*Einspänner*: black with whipped cream, served in a tall glass.
*Eiskaffee*: black with whipped cream and vanilla ice cream.
*Kapuziner*: cappuccino, topped with a dollop of whipped cream and sprinkled with powdered chocolate.
*Melange*: frothy and milky, maybe with a blob of whipped cream.
*Mocca*: strong and black, most often espresso.
*Türkischer*: boiling hot and sweet.
And all served with a glass of cold water with the spoon balanced on top, refilled by the waiter as soon as it is empty.

## Café Sacher

- Hotel Sacher
- Philharmonikerstrasse 4
- Daily 6.30 a.m.–11.30 p.m.

Very touristic but still quite cosy.

## Café Central

- Herrengasse 14 (Palais Ferstel)
- Monday to Saturday
- 8 a.m.–10 p.m.

The town's most famous literary café at the end of the 19th century counted Stefan Zweig and Leon Trotzky among its clients.

In the renovated splendour of the Palais Ferstel's stables, a statue of writer Peter Altenberg sits in one corner.

## Demel

- Kohlmarkt 14
- Daily 10 a.m.–7 p.m.

*The* Vienna pastry-shop, not to be missed. The shop-window is glorious (even more so at Christmas), the pastry selection irresistible. Try to get a table in the front room which, with its mirrors and décor, makes you feel as though you are sitting in your own monumental chocolate-box.

## Griensteidl

- Michaelerplatz 2
- Daily 8 a.m.–midnight

Another legendary literary café. Dignified subdued atmosphere.

## Hawelka

- Dorotheergasse 6
- Wednesday to Monday
- 8 a.m.–2 a.m.
- Sunday and public holidays
- 4 p.m.–2 a.m.

Still managed by the indefatigable Hawelka family. In the 1960s, a rendezvous for the avant-garde. The interior has remained unchanged, but the clientèle has become younger. Crowded after 10 p.m. when delicious fresh *Buchtel* are served (yeast buns with plum jam filling).

## Kleines Café

- Franziskanerplatz 3
- Monday to Saturday
- 10 a.m.–2 a.m.
- Sunday, public holidays
- 1 p.m.–2 a.m.

Small café, great charm, with interior design by Hermann Czech. Pleasant terrace in summer on the quiet Franziskanerplatz with its fountain and church.

## Landtmann

- Dr-Karl-Lueger-Ring 4
- Daily 8 a.m.–midnight

Next to the Burgtheater opposite City Hall. Extremely comfortable, this authentic bourgeois coffeehouse was a favourite haunt of Sigmund Freud. Spacious terrace in summer.

## Museum

- Friedrichstrasse 6
- Daily 8 a.m.–midnight

Unfortunately its original décor by Adolf Loos was destroyed in World War II. The café remains a popular meeting place for students and chess-players (in the back room).

## Prückel

- Stubenring 24
- Daily 9 a.m.–10 p.m.
- Summer terrace

The 1950s setting—and charm—have been preserved. Cakes are home-made, the choice of newspapers abundant and the formally dressed waiters first class. The back room is used for playing bridge.

## Schwarzenberg

- Kärntner Ring
- Daily 7 a.m.–midnight
- Fine summer terrace

Opposite Hotel Imperial, traditional coffeehouse, friendly service. During the carnival period, the café stays open to serve food from 2 to 6 a.m.

## Sperl

- Gumpendorferstrasse 11
- Monday to Saturday
  7 a.m.–11 p.m.
- Sunday and public holidays
  from 3 p.m.

Popular with billiard- and card-players. Home-made cakes, friendly service.

## Stein

- Wahringerstrasse 6-8
- Monday to Friday 7 a.m.–1 a.m.
- Sunday and public holidays
  from 9 a.m.

Catch up with your e-mail in this trendy Cyber-café. Simple and modern in design, opposite the Votivkirche, it's ideal for Sunday brunch.

## BARS

Following are a few addresses for night-owls. There are also countless bars in the so-called "Bermuda Triangle", the night-life district centering around Judengasse.

## Barfly's Club

- Hotel Fürst Metternich
- Esterhazygasse 33
- Daily 6 p.m.–3 a.m.

Endless selections of whiskies and rum. One of the town's most popular bars.

## Castillo

- Biberstrasse 8
- Monday to Saturday
  8 p.m.–3 a.m.
- Sunday to 2 a.m.

Quiet during the week, difficult to get a table at the weekend.

### First Floor

- Seitenstettengasse/Rabensteig
- Daily 7 p.m.–3 a.m.

Interesting cocktail bar with a huge aquarium.

### Havana Club-Salsothek

- Mahlerstrasse 11
- Daily 8 p.m.–5 a.m.

Latin American atmosphere: long salsa nights.

### KIX Bar

- Bäckerstrasse 4
- Daily 7 p.m.–2 a.m.
- Friday, Saturday to 3 a.m.

High walls in garish colours, minimalist furniture, more reminiscent of New York than Vienna. Very good cocktails.

### Krah Krah

- Rabensteig 4
- Monday to Saturday
- 11 p.m.–2 a.m.
- Sunday to 1 a.m.

Good selection of beers, tasty sandwiches. Casual atmosphere.

### Loos-Bar/American Bar

- Kärntner Strasse 10
- Summer: daily 6 p.m.–4 a.m.
- Winter: Monday to Saturday noon–4 a.m.

Tiny bar designed by Adolf Loos in 1908, a Jugendstil gem, protected monument since 1959.

### Miles Smiles

- Lange Gasse 51
- Monday to Thursday
- 8 p.m.–2 a.m.
- Friday, Saturday to 4 a.m.

Concerts for jazz fans.

### Onyx-Bar

- Haas-Haus, 6th floor
- Stephansplatz 12
- Monday to Saturday
- 4 p.m.–2 a.m.

Cocktail bar with view of Stephansdom.

### Palmenhaus im Burggarten

- Burgring/Albertina entrance
- Daily 10 p.m.–2 a.m.

Impressive setting, restaurant.

### Planters' Club

- Zelinkagasse 4
- Daily 5 p.m.–4 a.m.

Spacious bar in colonial style.

### Shulz

- Siebensterngasse 31
- Monday to Saturday 9 a.m.–2 a.m.
- Sunday from 5 p.m.

Sixties bar, bright and pleasant.

### Skybar

- Kärntner Strasse 19
- Steffl 7th floor
- Daily 11 a.m.–4 a.m.

This fashionable bar offers a magnificent city view.

## WINE GARDENS

Just like the coffeehouse, the *Heuriger* is a local institution, taking its name from the new white wine. The growers are permitted to sell a certain amount directly to the public. Do as the Viennese do and take a trip out to the outskirts of town to sip a glass or two in the open air and eat a simple meal. You will frequently be entertained by typical Viennese songs to the accompaniment of violin, guitar and accordion. The season runs from March to October.

### Bach-Hengl

Sandgasse 7–9
19th district, Döbling
Tram 38
Tel. 320 2439
Daily 4 p.m.–midnight
Wine has been produced here since the 12th century. Typical atmosphere.

### Fuhrgassl-Huber

Neustift am Walde 68
19th district, Döbling
Bus 35A
Tel. 440 1405
Monday to Saturday
2 p.m.–midnight
Sunday from noon
In winter, enjoy the comfort of this elegant restaurant tastefully furnished in wood. Self-service at hot and cold buffet.

### Sirbu

Kahlenberger Strasse 210
19th district, Döbling
Tram D
Tel. 320 5928
Monday to Saturday
3 p.m.–midnight
Closed mid-October to early April
One of the town's best Heuriger. The wine is very good.

### Weingut Werner Welser

Probusgasse 12
19th district, Döbling
Tel. 318 9797
Daily 3.30 p.m.–midnight
Copious buffet, various home-made strudels. Music.

### Wettig-Altes Winzerhaus

Bloschgasse 7
19th district, Kahlenberger Dorf
Tel. 375 420
Monday to Saturday
4 p.m.–11 p.m.
Sunday, public holidays from noon
Closed Tuesday
Garden with ................. ...
Leopoldsberg.

### Zum Weihrauch

Kaasgrabengasse 77
19th district, Döbling
Tel. 320 5818
Reservation recommended
Pretty garden, agreeable atmosphere, and good cooking

# Entertainment

As a capital of good living, Vienna offers plenty of opportunities for entertainment. To forget the rigours of winter, the Viennese brighten up their evenings with concerts, operas, theatre plays and intoxicating balls.

## Prater

Subway U1: Praterstern
Tram O, 5, 21: Praterstern
Volksprater (amusements)
April to September daily
8 a.m.–11 p.m.
Giant ferris wheel *(Riesenrad)*
May to September daily
9.30 a.m.–11 p.m.;
mid-February to April and
October to mid-November daily
10 a.m.–10 p.m.

Christmas and New Year's
holidays 11 a.m.–8 p.m.
This huge park, covering some
1,300 ha (526 acres), was the
emperor's hunting ground in the
16th century. Joseph II opened it up
to the public in 1766 and the Prater
became an amusement park for
young and old, with everything
from roller-coaster to ghost train.
The giant ferris wheel erected for
the World Exhibition of 1897 with

its famous red cabins dominates the whole park and offers a magnificent view of the city from a height of 65 m (213 ft) . The wheel was destroyed in World War II and restored in 1947. It achieved world fame in the film *The Third Man*. On the Praterhauptallee are also the Planetarium, the Ernst-Happel football stadium and the Lusthaus, a hunting lodge converted into a restaurant.

## THEATRE

*Wien-Programm*, the monthly listing of cultural events, is available at all tourist information offices and ticket offices.

### Akademietheater

⋮ Lisztstrasse 1
⋮ Subway U4: Stadtpark
⋮ Tel. 5144 42959/60

Excellent repertoire of classical and contemporary plays.

### Burgtheater

⋮ Dr-Karl-Lueger-Ring
⋮ Subway U2: Schottentor
⋮ Tram 1, 2: Burgtheater
⋮ Tel 5144 42959/60

The Burgtheater built in Italian Renaissance style in 1888 is considered by many to be the best theatre in the German-speaking world. It is claimed that the purest and best German is spoken here.

The programme ranges from the European and German classics to the parodies of 19th-century Viennese playwright Johann Nestroy.

### Ronacher

⋮ Seilerstätte 9
⋮ Tram 1, 2: Schwarzenbergplatz
⋮ Tel. 588 850

Authentic music hall with operettas and light theatre comedies.

---

### THEATRE TICKETS

The music season usually lasts from September 1 to June 30. It is advisable to make your reservations in writing at least three weeks in advance. Agencies charge a commission in the region of 20 per cent for seat reservation. However, you can book your tickets directly at the theatre or concert hall.

Ticket agency: Wien-Tickets, Linke Wienzeile 6. Open Monday to Friday 8 a.m.–6 p.m., Saturday, Sunday 9 a.m. to noon. Tel. 588 850.

For the theatres belonging to the Federal Theatre Association (*Bundestheaterverbund*), Akademietheater, Burgtheater, Staatsoper and Volkoper, commission-free sales offices at Hanuschgasse 3 and Goethegasse 1 open Monday to Friday 9 a.m.–6 p.m., Saturday 9 a.m.–noon. Tel. 5144 42960 for information. Credit cards accepted.

## Theater an der Wien

- Linke Wienzeile 6
- Subway U1, U2, U4: Karlsplatz
- Tel. 588 850

Playwright and actor Emanuel Schikaneder founded this theatre in 1801. The première of Mozart's *Magic Flute,* for which he had written the libretto, was performed ten years earlier on the same site near the entrance to the Naschmarkt, as was Beethoven's *Fidelio* in 1805. Today, the theatre stages large-scale musicals.

## Theater in der Josefstadt

- Josefstädter Strasse 26
- Tram J: Theater in der Josefstadt
- Tel. 4270 0300

The great director-producer Max Reinhardt worked in this theatre from 1920 to 1930. It opened in 1788. Productions here are often more popular in appeal than those of the Burgtheater and make a pleasant contrast with the classical décor.

## Schauspielhaus

- Porzellangasse 19
- Tram D: Porzellangasse
- Tel. 317 0101

The theatre founded in the 1970s for underground works today puts on plays by contemporary Austrian and foreign writers.

## Volkstheater

- Neustiftgasse 1
- Subway U2: Volkstheater
- Tel. 524 7263

This old theatre stages modern, avant-garde productions and operettas, but Shakespeare, too.

## Marionettentheater

- Schönbrunner Schloßstrasse 47
- 13th district
- Subway U4: Schönbrunn
- Tram 10, 48: Schönbrunn
- Tel. 817 3247

Acclaimed puppet theatre in the court wing of the palace.

## MUSIC

For many Viennese, concert-going is part of daily life. They dash straight from work to the concert hall, ever eager to hear, perhaps for the tenth time, a performance of Mozart's 41st Symphony. Afterwards they will avidly discuss the conductor's interpretation and the next concert date.

## Staatsoper

- opernring 1
- Subway U1, U2, U4: Karlsplatz
- Tram 1, 2, D or J: Oper
- Programme information:
- Tel. 5144 42959/60
- Telephone sales only
- by credit card

Tickets are put on sale one month before the performance (see also

p. 59). Remaining seats are sold at the opera house on the day of performance, from 10 a.m. until one hour before the curtain rises, and then the best standing-room tickets are sold. The Vienna Opera is the last opera house in the world with a permanent repertoire of some 150 works.

## Musikverein
- Bösendorferstrasse 12
- Subway U1, U2, U4: Karlsplatz
- Tram 1,2: Schwarzenbergplatz

---

### LET'S GO OUT TONIGHT

The Viennese are known for their fondness for etiquette and chivalry—Austria cultivates its traditions. If you want to be accepted, they should be respected. Dress decorously for opera, theatre and concerts. If you are attending a great ball like the Opera Ball, then white tie and tails for the gentleman and long evening dress for the lady are a must. Costume-hire (rental) shops can help you out if necessary. Here is a small selection:

Babsi's Kostümverleih, Gentzgasse 9 (8th district), tel. 479 6118;

Elite, Neustiftgasse 137/7 (7th district), tel. 523 5346;

Kaba Fundus, Amtshausgasse 7 (5th district), tel. 545 5866;

Lambert Hofer, Simmeringer Hauptstrasse 28, tel. 740 900.

---

- Ticket sales begin one month before concert date.
- Concert information:
- tel. 505 8190; fax 5058 68194
- Telephone sales by credit card only.
- Ticket sales at the concert hall:
- Monday to Friday 9 a.m.–6 p.m.;
- Saturday 9 a.m.–noon
- Open September 1–June 30

The New Year's Day concert broadcast all over the world begins on January 1 at 11 a.m. in the grand Goldener Saal, which is renowned for its outstanding acoustics. It seats 2,000. Ticket sales for the following New Year's concert begin on January 2. The Brahmssaal is used for chamber music recitals, with the Vienna Philharmonic holding 18 concerts each year.

## Volksoper
- Währingerstrasse 78
- Subway U6: Volksoper
- Tram 40, 41, 42: Volksoper
- Tel. 5144 42959/60
- Telephone-sales only by credit card

The "People's Opera", built in 1898 for the 50th anniversary of Franz Joseph's coronation, is devoted to operettas, and the occasional opera. Productions are first-rate but slightly less classical than at the Staatsoper.

## Wiener Konzerthaus

- Lothringer Strasse 40
- Subway U4: Stadtpark
- Tel. 712 1211
- Telephone sales by credit card only.
- Sale at the theatre Monday to Friday 9 a.m.–7.30 p.m.;
- Saturday till 1 p.m.

This handsome Jugendstil building was erected in 1912 by the Vienna Concert Society.

Symphonic music is performed in the Great Hall *(Grosser Saal)*, chamber music in the Mozart and Schubert halls. Concerts with world-famous soloists are outstanding in quality.

## Wiener Sängerknaben

- Hofburg: Burgkapelle
- (Schweizerhof entrance)
- Sunday mass 9.15 a.m. (except July, August)
- Advance booking essential
- Tel. 533 9927

The Wiener Sängerknaben boys' choir was founded in 1498 under Emperor Maximilian I. Their concerts were once reserved for select audiences. Joseph Haydn and Franz Schubert were both members of the choir.

The angel-voiced boys still wear sailor suits for performances, recalling the times when the empire had a powerful navy.

---

### CAPITAL OF MUSIC

Austrian music, subject to Mediterranean as well as Germanic influences, has always had a seductive elegance. The musical renown of Vienna lasted from the last third of the 18th century to the first half of the 20th, from Haydn to Webern. During this time an impressive series of great talents were active in Vienna: Gluck, Haydn, Mozart, Beethoven, Schubert, Strauss, Bruckner, Brahms, Mahler, Wolf, Schönberg, Berg and many others.

While it was completely taken with Italian composers in the 17th century, Vienna evolved in the second half of the 18th, with Haydn and Mozart, to Europe's music capital. Like the Esterhazy family, who commissioned symphonies and masses from Haydn, princes competed for the privilege of financing a composer who would in exchange dedicate to them some of their works. Johann Strauss transformed a plodding German dance into the gay, whirling waltz which started in popular dance halls and soon took the city by storm. His son, also Johann, became known as the Waltz King.

At the beginning of the 20th century, Gustav Mahler breathed new life into the town as conductor of the Philharmonic. With its 12-tone music, the Second Vienna School brought about a musical revolution.

# *Excursions*

We propose here four day trips from Vienna, revealing more rustic delights of the countryside away from the pomp and splendour of the capital. The first destination is close to the city and can be reached by subway or tram.

## KAHLENBERG

This walk takes you through the villages of Heiligenstadt, Nussdorf and Grinzing at the foot of Kahlenberg slope. If you have the time, the hike to the top is rewarded with a grand panoramic view.

## Heiligenstadt

- Subway U4: Heiligenstadt (terminus)
- Tram D to terminus

When you arrive in Heiligenstadt, take a look at the impressive Karl-Marx-Hof, a pioneering housing estate that stretches over 1 km and counts more than 1,600 apartments. It was built at the end of the 1920s by Karl Ehn, an important architect of Vienna's Social Democrat era, but still seems startlingly modern in appearance. Begin your walk in the footsteps of Beethoven, who lived at

Probusgasse 6. In this house, now set out as a small museum, the composer wrote his *Heiligenstädter Testament*, a letter to his brother in which he describes his increasing deafness and feeling of isolation.

## Nussdorf

Perched high over the Danube, the village boasts several nicely located Heuriger wine gardens. Operetta composer Franz Lehar owned a country mansion here, which is now open to the public.
Kahlenbergstrasse meanders up to the vineyards. The walk involves a little effort, but it is repaid with a stunning view over the Danube and Alps from the terrace of a restaurant at the top of the hill. You may also like to visit the Josefskirche with its pictures of the Turkish siege of 1683.

## Grinzing

A side trip on the way to the Kahlenberg goes to the pretty village of Grinzing, famous for its charming Heuriger wine gardens. Cobenzlgasse and Höhenstrasse offer an easy path up to the top of the Kahlenberg. Wander a while around the village to seek out its attractive houses and old wine presses. There's also an elegant late-Gothic church with a copper dome.

It is worth driving on to the Leopoldsberg as the view from there is splendid. This hill is named after Leopold III of Babenberg, founder of Klosterneuburg Abbey.

## THE WACHAU

Less than 100 km (60 miles) west of Vienna is the beautiful countryside of the Danube Valley. Castles and monasteries were built on rocky spurs high above the river.

## Klosterneuburg

⋮ 12 km (7.5 miles)
⋮ Rapid train *(Schnellbahn)*
⋮ Bus 238, 239

Leopold III of Babenberg founded this abbey *(Stift)* in the 12th century on the spot where, according to popular legend, his hunting dogs found the lost veil of his wife Agnes. Austria's first major Romanesque monastery was partially destroyed at the beginning of the 18th century. Karl VI had it rebuilt as a combination of palace and church. The imposing imperial staircase *(Kaiserstiege)* leads to the living quarters. Gothic and baroque paintings and sculptures are displayed in a museum.
Leave some time free to visit the frequently reconstructed basilica, St-Leopold-Kapelle, in which you can see the tomb of Leopold III, sanctified in the 15th century.

## Melk

- 100 km (60 miles) west of Vienna
- Autobahn (motorway) A1

The hilltop monastery of Melk towers majestically over the town. It was the seat of the Babenberg family since the 10th century. Leopold III handed the castle over to the Benedictines who built it into a fortified monastery. At the end of the 18th century it was rebuilt in baroque style by Abbot Dietmayr. With its symmetrical towers and central dome, the church dominates the ensemble of monastery buildings. Frescoes and gold and marble ornament characterize the decoration.

## WIENERWALD

The Vienna Woods offer splendid opportunities for exploring the hinterland. The scenery in these last foothills of the Alps is very romantic, perfect for long walks beneath the pine trees, their needles crackling underfoot.

## Heiligenkreuz

- 30 km (19 miles) southwest of Vienna
- Autobahn A21
- Bus 265 from Südtirolerplatz

The Cistercian monastery of Heiligenkreuz was founded by Burgundian monks on behalf of Leopold III of Babenberg in 1135. It was named for what is believed to be a piece of the Holy Cross, brought back from the Holy Land by Leopold himself and now kept in the monastery. You can visit the Romanesque church, monastery and chapter-house, with 13th-century stained-glass windows.

## Mayerling

- 36 km (22.5 miles) southwest of Vienna
- Autobahn A21

This peaceful little market town became known through the tragic event which shook the empire at the end of the 19th century. Crown Prince Archduke Rudolf, who was married to Stephanie of Belgium, shared the liberal ideas of his mother, Empress Elisabeth. He supported the demands of the Hungarian parliamentary opposition and so set a large part of the Austro-Hungarian aristocracy against him. He fell in love with the 17-year-old Baroness Mary Vetsera and asked for his marriage with Stephanie to be annulled by the pope. Rudolf's father Franz Joseph was against it and demanded an end to the adulterous love affair. On January 28, 1889, Rudolf killed his mistress in his hunting lodge and then committed suicide. Franz Joseph had a Carmelite convent built on the site of the lodge.

## Baden

- 26 km (16 miles) south of Vienna
- Autobahn A2
- Rapid train *(Schnellbahn)* from the Staatsoper

The site of this charming town was already known in Roman times for its hot sulphur springs. In the 19th century the imperial court came regularly to take the waters at the elegant spa resort. Beethoven lived at Rathausgasse 10. You can use the thermal baths or try your luck at the casino.

## BURGENLAND

This is Austria's easternmost province, on the border with Hungary. It boasts Europe's largest steppe lake, the Neusiedler See, and is also renowned for its wines. The provincial capital is Eisenstadt. It is relatively flat, and therefore great for hikers and cyclists.

## Neusiedler See

- 60 km (37 miles) southeast of Vienna
- Autobahn A4

The lake is part of the Neusiedlersee-Seewinkel National Park. The reserve covers some 14,000 ha (34,600 acres) of Austrian and Hungarian territory and is blessed with abundant flora and fauna. The shallow, slightly salty lake, entirely fed by groundwater, is ringed by a belt of reeds in which more than 300 species of birds live and breed—heron, wild geese, egret, and over 60 couples of nesting storks.

On the east shore, make a stop at the little town of Rust, protected as a national monument with its picturesque houses, two dozen vineyards and its Fischerkirche, the fishermen's church. In July and August, the townsfolk live in huts built on stilts, linked to each other by wooden bridges.

In Mörbisch, 3 km (2 miles) from Rust, the dazzling white houses decorated with flowers and corncobs evoke the villages of nearby Hungary. A road through the water-reeds leads to a pretty bathing area. From mid-July to the end of August, this enchanting region hosts an operetta festival.

## Eisenstadt

- Southeast of Vienna
- Autobahn (motorway) A3

Visit the former palace and winter residence of the Esterhazy family, in particular the ceremonial hall where Haydn wrote most of his masterpieces. In summer you can sit out at one of the terrace cafés on the traffic-free main street. The frescoes on the city hall and the 18th-century house façades are of remarkable beauty.

# The Hard Facts

## Airport
The international Vienna-Schwechat airport lies about 20 km (12.5 miles) southeast of the city centre. There is a tourist information office (open 8.30 a.m.–9 p.m.) as well as the major car rental companies. Buses of the Vienna Airport Lines company and rapid trains run regularly and often to offer a fast and uncomplicated link with the city centre.

Airport tel. 700 70
Airport information
tel. 700 2233
Bus information
tel. 5800 33369

## Bicycles
Cycle lanes are common in the city centre, notably around the Ring. Bikes can be rented at railway stations.

## City Tours
To hire an English-speaking tour guide tel. 440 3094. Tours are organized on specific themes, such as Jugendstil architecture and design. Enquire at the tourist information office, Kärntner Strasse 38. Vienna Sightseeing Tours:
tel. 7124 6830
Tours in an old-fashioned tram, May to October:
tel. 7909 44026

Boat cruises May to October, DDSG Blue Danube:
tel. 727 500

## Climate
Vienna has a continental climate. Winters are often harsh, with occasional snow. In January and February, the temperature may drop to –15°C (–9°F). In summer it may climb to 30°C (86°F).

## Crime
By and large, Vienna is a safe city. Nonetheless, do not flaunt your valuables carelessly in crowded places. If you lose your passport or identity cards, contact your embassy or consulate (see address below).

## Driving
Seat-belts are compulsory. Children under 12 must sit in the back in special safety seats.

Driving on the motorway requires a special permit which can be bought for one or two weeks or for a whole year. The speed limit on the motorway is 130 kph (80 mph), on country highways 100 kph (60 mph) and in town 50 kph (30 mph).

Parking in town is permitted only in designated zones. Regulatory parking discs can be purchased in tobacco shops

*(Trafik)*, the post office or in railway stations.

## Embassies and Consulates
**Canada**:
 Laurenzerberg 2
 1010 Vienna
 Tel. 531 38 3000
**Eire**:
 Landstrasser Hauptstrasse 2
 1030 Vienna
 Tel. 715 42 460
**UK**:
 Jauresgasse 12
 1030 Vienna
 Tel. (embassy) 713 1575
 Tel. (consulate) 714 6117
**US embassy**:
 Boltzmanngasse 16
 1090 Vienna
 Tel. 313 39
**US consulate**:
 Gartenbaupromenade 2
 1010 Vienna
 Tel. 313 39

## Emergencies
**Police**: 133
**Fire**: 122
**Ambulance**: 144
**Emergency doctor**: 141

## Entrance Formalities
Austria is a member of the European Union (EU) and signatory of the Schengen Agreement. If you are a citizen of an EU country, you should nonetheless take a valid passport or identity card. Travellers from non-EU countries may import, duty-free, 200 cigarettes, 100 cigarillos, 50 cigars or 250 g tobacco, 1 litre of spirits or 2 litres of wine.

## Fiaker Cabs
These open coaches drawn by two horses have been trotting through the streets of Vienna for over 300 years. Fiaker ranks are stationed at several major tourist locations, notably Michaelerplatz and Stephansplatz. Agree on the price before setting out.

## Handicapped Visitors
Tourist information offices distribute a brochure Vienna for Handicapped Visitors *(Wien für Gäste mit Handicap)*. Enquire beforehand by telephone to see if a monument or museum offers wheelchair-access.

## Lost Property
The lost property office is at Wasagasse 22, 9th district, Monday to Friday 8 a.m.–noon; tel. 313 440

## Money
The Austrian Schilling (ÖS or ATS) is divided into 100 Groschen (g). Coins: 10, 50 g, and 1, 5, 10 and 20 ÖS; notes from 20 to 5,000 ÖS.

 The city centre has plenty of automatic cash-distributors. Most restaurants and hotels accept credit cards.

The Euro comes into operation January 2002. One euro = 13.7603 ÖS.

## Opening Hours

*Pharmacy*: 8 a.m.–noon and 2 p.m.–6 p.m.

*Banks and currency exchange offices*: Monday to Friday 8 or 9 a.m.–3 or 3.30 p.m. Small offices close 12.30–1.30 p.m.

*Shops*: generally Monday to Friday 9 a.m.–6.30 p.m., Saturday 9 a.m.–5 p.m.

*Post office*: The main post office, Fleischmarkt 19, is open permanently. Other branches: Monday to Friday 8 a.m.–noon and 2 p.m.–6 p.m.

## Public Holidays

| | |
|---|---|
| January 1 | *Neujahrstag* New Year's Day |
| January 6 | *Heilige Drei Könige* Twelfth Night |
| May 1 | *Tag der Arbeit* Labour Day |
| August 15 | *Mariä Himmelfahrt* Assumption |
| October 26 | *Nationalfeiertag* National Holiday |
| November 1 | *Allerheiligen* All Saints' Day |
| December 8 | *Mariä Empfängnis* Immaculate Conception |
| December 25 | *Weihnachten* Christmas Day |
| December 26 | *Stefanitag* St Stephen's Day |

Movable holidays:

| | |
|---|---|
| Easter Monday | *Ostermontag* |
| Ascension Day | *Auffahrt* |
| Whit Monday | *Pfingstmontag* |
| Corpus Christi | *Fronleichnam* |

*Fasching* (Carnival) begins November 11 at 11.11 a.m. and lasts till Ash Wednesday; the Ball season "proper" begins with the *Kaiserball* (Emperor's Ball) December 31. More than 200 balls are held, and most are open to outsiders.

The music season begins in September. Ask at tourist information offices for detailed programmes.

In December, the city is bedecked with decorations, Christmas trees are set up in Schönbrunn park and in front of city hall, and there's a traditional Christmas market.

## Public Transport

The Vienna subway *(U-Bahn)* and tramway operate efficiently. The subway is open from 5.30 a.m. to midnight. Comprehensive information is available at the Karlsplatz subway office. At street level, station are indicated by signs with a white U on a blue background.

The *Wien-Karte* is a cut-rate ticket permitting unlimited travel on subway, tram and bus for 72 hours. The same ticket gives you discounts at many museums, shops and restaurants. It can be purchased in hotels, tourist information offices or public transport sales offices. Tobacco shops *(Trafik)* sell day tickets *(Tageskarte)* and 7-day tickets *(Wochenkarten)*. These tickets must be punched in a machine the first time they are used.

Children under 6 travel free; under-15s pay half price and travel free on Sunday, public holidays and school holidays.

## Taxis

They can be hailed on the street or ordered by phone: 31300, 1715, 1731 or 319 2511.

Rates are higher at night from 11 p.m. to 6 a.m., and on Sundays and public holidays. Trips between the city centre and Wien-Schwechat airport have a set price, which you should check before you set off.

## Telephone

Telephone cabins take coins or phone-cards—available at tobacco shops *(Trafik)*—and a few accept international credit cards.

Rates are cheaper between 8 p.m. and 8 a.m. and from Friday 6 p.m. to Monday 8 a.m.
Information: tel. 1611
For Europe: 1613
Other countries: 1614

## Tipping

Over and above the official service charge most often included in the bill, it is customary to leave a tip of 10–15 per cent in hotels, restaurants and cafés.

## Toilets

Public toilets cost 1 or 5 Schillings and are generally open 9 a.m.–7 p.m. Some restaurant or coffeehouse facilities also require a small tip to the attendant.

## Tourist Information Offices

Friedrichstr. 7, 9 a.m.–7 p.m.
Tel. 588 000

Kärntner Str. 38, 9 a.m.–7 p.m.
tel. 513 8892

Wiener Tourismusverband
Obere Augartenstrasse 40
Tel. 211 140

ÖAMTC (Automobile Club)
Traffic information
Schubertring 1–3
Tel. 711 990

Internet information
http://info.wien.at

## Trains

Timetable information is available by tel. 58 000. This applies to trains for West- and Süd-bahnhof, Wien Mitte, Wien Nord and Franz-Josephsbahnhof.

# INDEX

# The Top Ten

This guide describes the most interesting architectural monuments, museums and parks and the best shops, coffeehouses and restaurants. If you have only two or three days to visit Vienna, then make your pick of our "favourites".

- Breakfast with a view of the garden of the Palais Schwarzenberg (p. 52)
- See the city from the ferris wheel in the Prater (p. 58)
- Visit the imperial apartments in the Hofburg (pp. 27–28)
- Delight in the perfect elegance of the Lippizaner horses at the Spanish Riding School (p. 29)
- Savour a coffee and cake at Demel (p. 54)
- Admire the Great Masters exhibited at the Akademie der bildenden Künste (p. 38)
- Walk in the lovely park of Schloss Schönbrunn (p. 46)
- Read the international press in Café Central (p. 54)
- Sample the wines in Grinzing (p. 64)
- Revel in the unspoiled nature of the Neusiedler See (p. 66)

General editor: Barbara Ender-Jones
Design: Aude Aquoise
Photos: Renata Holzbachová
Maps: JPM Publications

Copyright © 2000 JPM Publications S.A.
12, avenue William-Fraisse, 1006 Lausanne, Suisse
E-mail: information@jpmguides.com
Internet: http://www.jpmguides.com/

Every care has been taken to verify the information in the guide, but the publisher cannot accept responsibility for any errors that may have occurred. If you spot an inaccuracy or a serious omission, please let us know.

Printed in Switzerland — Weber/Bienne (CTP)

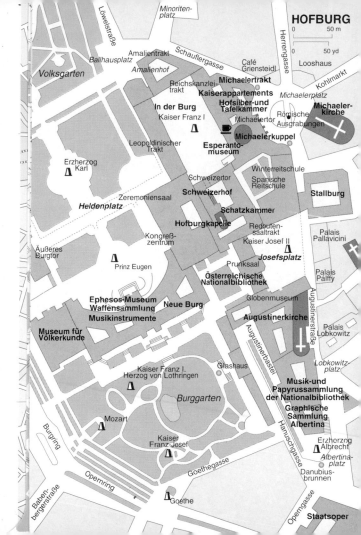

# HOFBURG

0 — 50 m
0 — 50 yd

*Löwelstraße*

*Minoritenplatz*

*Schauflergasse*

*Herrengasse*

Looshaus

Café Griensteidl

*Ballhausplatz*

*Amalientrakt*

*Amalienhof*

*Volksgarten*

Reichskanzleitrakt

**Michaelertrakt**

**Kaiserappartements**

**Hofsilber- und Tafelkammer**

*Michaelerplatz*

**Michaelerkirche**

**In der Burg**

Kaiser Franz I

Michaelertor

Römische Ausgrabungen

**Michaelerkuppel**

Leopoldinischer Trakt

**Esperanto-museum**

Erzherzog Karl

Winterreitschule

Spanische Reitschule

**Stallburg**

Zeremoniensaal

Schweizertor

**Schweizerhof**

*Heldenplatz*

**Schatzkammer**

**Hofburgkapelle**

Redoutensaaltrakt

Kaiser Josef II

Palais Pallavicini

Kongreß-zentrum

*Josefsplatz*

Prunksaal

Palais Pálffy

*Äußeres Burgtor*

Prinz Eugen

**Österreichische Nationalbibliothek**

**Epheros-Museum Waffensammlung Musikinstrumente**

**Neue Burg**

Globenmuseum

**Augustinerkirche**

Palais Lobkowitz

**Museum für Völkerkunde**

Glashaus

*Augustinerbastei*

*Lobkowitz-platz*

Kaiser Franz I. Herzog von Lothringen

*Burggarten*

**Musik- und Papyrussammlung der Nationalbibliothek**

**Graphische Sammlung Albertina**

Mozart

Kaiser Franz-Josef

Erzherzog Albrecht

*Albertina-platz*

*Burgring*

Goethe

*Opernring*

Danubius-brunnen

*Opergasse*

*Goethegasse*

*Hanuschgasse*

*Bären-bergerstraße*

**Staatsoper**

Kohlmarkt

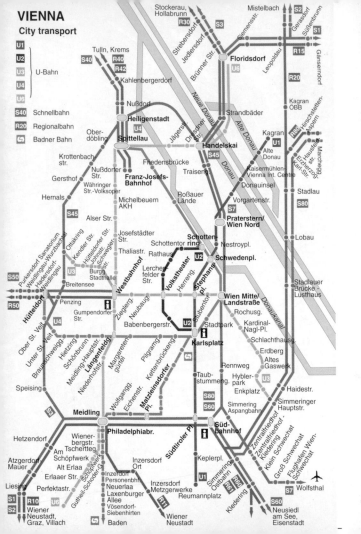